T0329105

# Cambridge Elements ≡

Elements in Religion and Monotheism
edited by
Paul K. Moser
*Loyola University Chicago*
Chad Meister
*Bethel University*

# DIVINE IDEAS

Thomas M. Ward
*Baylor University*

CAMBRIDGE
UNIVERSITY PRESS

# CAMBRIDGE
### UNIVERSITY PRESS

University Printing House, Cambridge CB2 8BS, United Kingdom

One Liberty Plaza, 20th Floor, New York, NY 10006, USA

477 Williamstown Road, Port Melbourne, VIC 3207, Australia

314–321, 3rd Floor, Plot 3, Splendor Forum, Jasola District Centre, New Delhi – 110025, India

79 Anson Road, #06–04/06, Singapore 079906

Cambridge University Press is part of the University of Cambridge.

It furthers the University's mission by disseminating knowledge in the pursuit of education, learning, and research at the highest international levels of excellence.

www.cambridge.org
Information on this title: www.cambridge.org/9781108819695
DOI: 10.1017/9781108876445

First published 2020

A catalogue record for this publication is available from the British Library.

ISBN 978-1-108-81969-5 Paperback
ISSN 2631-3014 (online)
ISSN 2631-3006 (print)

# Divine Ideas

Elements in Religion and Monotheism

DOI: 10.1017/9781108876445
First published online: August 2020

Thomas M. Ward
*Baylor University*
Author for correspondence: Thomas M. Ward, thomasmward@gmail.com

**Abstract:** This Element defends a version of the classical theory of divine ideas: the containment exemplarist theory of divine ideas. The classical theory holds that God has ideas of all possible creatures, that these ideas partially explain why God's creation of the world is a rational and free personal action, and that God does not depend on anything external to himself for having the ideas he has. The containment exemplarist version of the classical theory holds that God's own nature is the exemplar of all possible creatures, and therefore that God's ideas of possible creatures are in some sense ideas of himself. Containment exemplarism offers a monotheism fit for metaphysics, insofar as it is coherent, simple, and explanatorily powerful; and offers a metaphysics fit for monotheism, insofar as it leaves God truly worthy of the unconditional worship which Christians, along with Jews and Muslims, aspire to offer to God.

**Keywords:** God, worship, abstract objects, creation, divine ideas

ISBNs: 9781108819695 (PB), 9781108876445 (OC)
ISSNs: 2631-3014 (online), 2631-3006 (print)

# Contents

1  The Theory of Divine Ideas                    1

2  Theory and Worship                            8

3  Making Stuff Up                              14

4  Imitation of God                             22

5  Simple Enough                                30

6  Finding All Things in God                    39

7  The Metaphysics of Participation             48

8  No Secular Truths                            55

   Appendix                                     65

   References                                    66

   Acknowledgments                              73

# 1 The Theory of Divine Ideas

## 1.1 Creation

The heart of the doctrine of creation is that the existence of the world is due to a divine, and therefore personal, action: thinking and loving stand at the back of all things. This Element is about *the theory of divine ideas*, which is a traditional way of making sense of the doctrine of creation. The theory of divine ideas holds that God has ideas of all the creatures he could create, indeed has ideas of whole worlds of creatures he could create, and his actual creation of a world is sort of like an artist who, inspired by an idea of a painting she would like to paint, paints it. However, unlike the human artist, who has to reach outside herself to gather the stock of ideas on which her creativity depends, God has his ideas just from himself. Divine ideas are exemplars of God's creatures, and God himself is the exemplar of his ideas of creatures. God is the only totally original artist.

## 1.2 Ancient Origins

The theory of divine ideas is very old. Its classical expression is an artifact of the meeting of worlds, or worldviews: on the one hand, Greek philosophy with its Platonic Forms; and, on the other, Jewish theology with its monotheistic doctrine of creation. Greek philosophical influence on Jewish thought probably began as early as the third century BC when the Hebrew Bible was translated into Greek, the translation known as the Septuagint. Hints of a theory of divine ideas are to be found scattered in the Septuagint, and especially in its apocryphal books, in which God's Word (*Logos*) or Wisdom (*Sophia*) are personified as the agents of creation (Sir. 42:15, Wis. 9:1–2). But the standard narrative credits a later source, the Jewish philosopher Philo of Alexandria (d. 50 AD), with the first explicit synthesis of Jewish creation and Platonism.[1] Plato (d. *c*.347 BC) had envisioned a nonspatiotemporal realm of Forms, which are the exemplars of sensible things here below, the true realities which the things of this world but dimly reflect.[2] Philo reimagined these Forms as God's Ideas or Word(s), the exemplars by which God creates the heavens and earth. It is hard to overstate the influence of this basic picture on subsequent philosophical theology in the Abrahamic traditions, and especially in Christianity.

Yet it would be a mistake to think of the divine ideas tradition merely as an artifact of this Greco–Jewish synthesis. Judaism had its own theology of the

---

[1] Philo, *Creation of the World* IV–VI; Wolfson, *Philo*, vol. 1, pp. 200–204.
[2] Plato, *Timaeus* 27d–31b; *Phaedo* 100b–102b [see Cooper (ed.), *Complete Works*, for all citations].

Word (*Dabar*) which predates the Septuagint.[3] The word of the Lord made the heavens (Ps. 33:6) and the word of the Lord healed his people (Ps. 107:20). From the fourth century BC onward this native theology of the word was magnified within the liturgical context of spoken Aramaic glosses on the Hebrew Bible, glosses which saturated the Hebrew scriptures with the creative and sustaining activity of God's Word (*Memra*).[4] And Greek philosophical theology, independent of Judaism, had its own trajectory toward a theory of divine ideas – or at least toward a vision of a god who is an eternal mind containing in itself the intelligible structure of all things.[5] When the Stoic philosopher Seneca (d. 65 AD) gave clear voice to a straightforward monotheistic theory of divine ideas, it's as though the view had already become obvious,[6] and it is taken for granted in the second century syncretistic esotericism of the *Chaldean Oracles*[7] and the *Corpus Hermeticum*.[8] As Christian theologians were developing their own, Christ-centered theories of the divine ideas, the great pagan Neoplatonist philosophers advanced the new tradition of identifying Plato's Forms – most of them, anyway – as divine thoughts.[9]

## 1.3 Really Ancient Origins

But there is nothing originally Greek or Jewish in this core idea of one god who creates everything besides himself by means of his thoughts. Probably not by their oldest, third millennium theologies,[10] but still long, long ago, Egyptian religious thinkers had conceived of creation as the intellectual product of a single god.[11] Akhenaten (d. *c.*1334 BC), the famous fourteenth-century monotheist, composed a great Hymn to his god, Aten, which teaches the doctrine of creation ex nihilo and bears more than superficial resemblance to Psalm 104.[12] A text from the thirteenth century features the god Ptah, who conceives other gods and the created world in his heart, and then speaks them into being with his tongue – unaided by any primordial elements.[13] Another text from the thirteenth century speculates that all the gods' identity is "hidden in Amun"; the Sun is his face, Ptah is his body, and everything comes from the

---

[3] Carson, *Gospel According to John*, pp. 114–116.

[4] Ronning, *Targums and John's Logos Theology*, pp. 1–69; McNamara, *Targum and Testament*, pp. 41–92.

[5] Dillon, *Roots of Platonism*, pp. 35–49; Dillon, *The Middle Platonists*, pp. 126–129.

[6] Seneca, Epistle to Luculius 65.   [7] *Chaldean Oracles* fr. 37.   [8] *Corpus Hermeticum* I. 31.

[9] Plotinus, *Enneads* 5.5.2–3; Proclus, *Elements of Theology* 170.

[10] PT 527, 600, in Faulkner, *Pyramid Texts*, pp. 198, 246; Allen, *Genesis in Egypt*, pp. 13–14.

[11] Assmann, *Search for God*, pp. 189–198.

[12] "Hymn to Aton," in Foster, *Hymns, Prayers, and Songs*, pp. 102–107; Hoffmeier, *Akhenaten and the Origins of Monotheism*, pp. 245–266.

[13] "The Memphite Theology," in Lichtheim, *Ancient Egyptian Literature* I, pp. 54–55; Allen, *Genesis in Egypt*, pp. 43.

mouth of Amun[14] – one among many examples of the Egyptian theological penchant for unifying their many gods.[15]

Babylonian authors did not care very much about their original creator gods, Tiamat and Apsu. They cared far more about gods who were present and active in world affairs. But here too we find a sort of convergence of many gods upon one god, like Ptah or Amun, one god who has the power if not to create, then simply to be all the other gods. Thus, in the third millennium epic *Enuma Elish*, when Marduk establishes order in the world by his heroic deeds, the fifty great gods "take their seats" and praise Marduk with fifty names.[16] In a later text, probably from the fifteenth century or earlier, other gods appear to be no longer merely deferential to Marduk; instead they are identified with him, one god making shift for many.[17] If Egyptian metaphysical speculation converged upon a single divine origin of all, Babylonian religious devotion converged upon a single divine object of worship.

## 1.4 The Hebrew Bible

The Hebrew Bible engages these and other ancient theologies in several ways. It combines the Babylonian theme of heroic divine agency with the Egyptian impulse to adore the first principle of all things. It tells the story of the Israelites sometimes trying and frequently failing to reject foreign gods in favor of the exclusive worship of the one God. But it is also a proclamation that God, The LORD, on his own does divinity better than any pantheon and better than any chief of a pantheon and is therefore entitled to exclusive worship. He assumes all the qualities of the gods who were his rivals for the allegiance of his chosen people, and even takes the name of El, patriarch of the Canaanite pantheon.[18]

One side of this sole allegiance to God is entirely negative: you shall have no other gods but The LORD (Ex. 20:3). The altars of Baal and the fertility poles of Asherah must be torn down and must never be erected (Judg. 6:25; Deut. 12:3). This negativity eventually takes the ultimate form of denial that such rivals even exist: you must carry your idols, says God, but I will carry you (Is. 46:1–4). Whatever divine beings or members of the heavenly host there really are – those who shout for joy when God establishes the heavens, for example (Job

---

[14] Papyrus Leiden I 350, ch. 300, ll. 2–5, 14–15, in Allen, *Genesis in Egypt*, p. 54.

[15] Hornung, *Conceptions of God in Ancient Egypt*, pp. 86–99.

[16] *Enuma Elish*, in Arnold and Beyer, *Ancient Near East*, pp. 31–50; Heidel, *Babylonian Genesis*, p. 12; Lambert, *Babylonian Creation Myths*, pp. 3–4.

[17] Smith, *Origins of Biblical Monotheism*, pp. 87–88. Lambert, *Babylonian Creation Myths*, pp. 264–265. Assmann, *Of God and Gods*, pp. 62.

[18] Smith, *Early History of God*, pp. 32–43; Parke-Taylor, *Yahweh*, p. 37.

38:6–7) – are his creatures (Neh. 9:6), angels if you like, not to be worshipped as gods.

But there is a positive side to this sole allegiance, which is that the one God fulfills everything worth seeking in rival gods. Like Marduk, The LORD God assumes all divine qualities worth having. The benefit of being a god who can hide himself (Is. 45:15) and a god of which there must be no graven image (Deut. 4:15–19) is that he can reveal himself nearly any way he likes. God has just one true name but it is capacious as can be; God will be whatever he needs to be to accomplish his purposes (Ex. 3:14): a still small voice for Elijah (1 Kings 19:11) but a whirlwind for Job (Job 38:1).

Like Marduk and Baal, he is a warrior to whom the sea monster is but a fish which God draws forth from the waters for sport (Job 41:1–2; Ps. 104:26). Like Ptah, he is the architect and engineer of the world, establishing order (Job 38:4–6, 31–33). Like Baal, he is the god of weather (Ps. 18:6–15). Amun-Re and Aten have been eclipsed by the sun which is The LORD (Ps. 84:11), the Sun who makes the sun and everything else (Ps. 104:19). He is a husband who cares for his people (Is. 54:5), and they are bride enough for him; he needs no goddess to be his consort (Hos. 2:21–25).[19] But anything you might want in a goddess is already in God: he is a fierce mama bear (Hos. 13:8), a comforting mother (Is. 66:13), the one who gave birth to you (Deut. 32:18).[20] If zoolatry is your thing, God is, in addition to a bear, a lion (Is. 38:13), a leopard (Hos. 13:7), a bull (Num. 24:8), and – depending on your view about what it would take for someone to be the Messiah – a lamb (Is. 53:7).

The Hebrew Bible is not a record of the first monotheism, or the first doctrine of creation ex nihilo, or even the first inkling of the theory of divine ideas – that title goes to whomever wrote that bit about Ptah thinking up the whole world in his heart – but it records a monotheism the one God of which is so busy, so complicated, so rich, that it feels hardly innovative to say, in Greek terms, that this one God contains in himself the intelligible principles of everything that can be. Having read the Bible, what else would we expect of God?

## 1.5 God Before Creation

But the main point of this Element is not to consider the theory of divine ideas as an historical artifact but as a theory, a rational account of the way things are. What this theory is, first and foremost, is an account of God's rationality in creating the world. The account makes God the unique first principle of all, makes his creative activity intelligible and purposeful, and thereby makes his world the product of a mind and so able to be investigated rationally.

---

[19] Rabinowitz, *Faces of God*, pp. 83–88.  [20] Smith, *Early History of God*, pp. 48–52.

God, so the theory goes, is not only powerful enough to cause the existence of the world, but he is personal, with the powers distinctive of a person and a person with the best sort of character. From his personal powers we infer that God is rational and free, and from his perfect character we infer that he is good, wise, loving, just, merciful, and so on. Religious philosophers have of course attempted to reason retroactively, so as to arrive at this revealed conception of God by the tools of reason. Either by reason or revelation, or both, the theory of divine ideas only has rational traction once we are prepared to take as given that the world has in fact been made by such a creator, and not a generic First Cause.

If such a God is personal, then his actions are personal actions, and this means they are intentional and free; and if such a God is perfect in character, then his actions are rational and good. These guideposts for reflection on the doctrine of creation force us to think of God as knowing what he is doing when he creates. When he says, for example, "Let there be light (*Gen.* 1:3),"[21] he does not discover what light is when it comes into existence. He meant light. And if he meant it, then he knew about light *before* he spoke it into being.

The precise sense of 'before' is difficult to pin down; minimally, it is an explanatory or logical 'before'. If the world is a product of God's rational action then when God makes light he makes it, in part, *because* he knows about light, as when we say that the child aced the test *because* she knew her multiplication table. Knowing about light is part of the explanation of making light, and I mean 'before' just in that minimal sense of being a part of an explanation. And while I will not argue the claim here, I think this sort of 'before' is compatible with God being timeless.

## 1.6 Having in Mind

So God knows about creatures he creates before he creates them. What might it mean for God to know about creatures that do not yet exist? *We* know about creatures because they are already there among us for us to experience them. Once we've experienced them, we can take them around with us, in mind, thinking about them even when we are not experiencing them, as I take around my family in my mind when I travel. Knowing creatures by experiencing them obviously presupposes that there are already creatures to be studied. But this cannot be what we mean when we say that God knows about creatures before he makes any, because before he makes any, there aren't any: no land or seas, sun

---

[21] Biblical quotations throughout are taken from the Revised Standard Version of *The New Oxford Annotated Bible.*

and moon, fishes and birds, unless God makes them. So God must know about such things before he makes them.

It is very tricky to talk sense when we're trying to say what it is God is thinking about when we imagine him thinking about something which does not exist, and this is just the situation we're in when we are trying to think about what was in God's mind when he said "Let there be light." My own view is the scriptural view that God *is* light (1 Jn. 1:5), so that what God is thinking about when he thinks about light before created light is himself. But for now, don't focus on the object of God's thinking when he has something in mind; just focus on having in mind.

There are a few ordinary ways we talk about having something in mind. First, there is the quasi-sensory experience of seeing (hearing, etc.) in your head or mind, like when you have a song in your head or you are picturing a painting in your mind.

Second, we can have something in mind through a definition, as when we think about the triangle in terms of its definition or necessary properties, e.g., a figure with exactly three interior angles which equal 180 degrees. We might picture the words of a definition, or even picture something representing the thing defined, but these picturings are incidental to the experience of having the defined thing in mind.

Third, we also talk about having things in mind when expressing an intention or a preference. I say, "Let's do lunch"; you reply, "Sure, what did you have in mind?" I go on, "In-n-Out. That's a really good burger." Maybe I am picturing a cheeseburger when I say this. But this picturing is incidental to, or at best one component of, having In-n-Out in mind when it is in mind as a preference or intention. When it is in mind in this way I have some serious interest in making my idea a reality.

Fourth, another sort of action-oriented having in mind concerns things we know how to do. Your teacher gives you a calculus lesson. She asks, "Did you get all that?" You say, "Why yes, I think I do." She has helped you get something in mind, something in the calculus-shaped hole in your mind, and whatever this something is, it is what you have in mind when you do calculus or when you are aware of yourself as knowing calculus.

I see no reason to deny of God any of these ways of having in mind. If we've got as far as ascribing personhood and character to God, it's no stretch to ascribe to him these various abilities to picture, understand, prefer, intend, or do things he has in mind. Arguably, they're wrapped up in what it is to be personal, such that if it is viciously naive or anthropomorphic to think of God as having things in mind, then thinking of God as personal is, too.

If we're imagining God, so to speak, in the brainstorming phase of creation – something like considering his options – then naturally we will be thinking of him as having things in mind in the first two of the four ways; in the selection phase, the third way; and in the execution phase, the fourth way. I do not plan to rely on this division of ways of having in mind or to carefully distinguish different ways at different phases of God's creative action. The broader point is that there are obvious (if not fully understood) ways in which we have things in mind, and if we are to think of God as personal, then we must think of him as having things in mind in some ways which are intelligible to us given our own experience of having things in mind.

## 1.7 Divine Idea

A divine idea is a thing God has in mind. God thinks about himself and does so perfectly; so he has himself in mind – that is to say, has an idea of himself. If there are such things as parts or aspects of God, God knows these too, and perfectly; so he has ideas of his aspects or parts. God thinks about all the things he could make, the individuals, the types, the combinations of individuals and types, the histories, the worlds; so he has ideas of all these. This is the foundation of the theory of divine ideas: God is a personal creator perfect in character. He knows what he's doing when he does anything; his knowledge comes before his doing; and his knowledge is a matter of having in mind, and so having divine ideas, of all the things.

## 1.8 Total Originality

So God has things in mind and has creatures – possible creatures – in mind before he creates anything. It is important to emphasize the similarity between God's having things in mind and our having things in mind, in order to preserve the coherence of thinking of God as a person. But, naturally, there are some important differences between the way God has things in mind and the way we do. God, so I assert here but as I will argue in what follows, is *totally original*, and no human being, even the most creative human artist, is totally original.

Creative as she is, there are at least two ways in which the human artist cannot be totally original. First, to make, say, a painting, she requires some medium: canvas and paint. The quality of the painting will be determined not just by the skill and care the artist puts into its making, but also partially determined by the nature of the medium itself. Good paint and canvas make for better paintings than bad paint and canvas, all else being equal.

Second, while the idea of the painting might itself be a novel assemblage of simpler ideas, never thought up by any other human artist, the mind of the artist must be shaped by her interaction with the world – observing it with her senses, sharing it with human communities – to achieve that medium of concepts or language, habits or skills required for thinking up the idea of the painting. So we might say that the painting depends on a *material* medium, and that coming up with the idea of the painting depends on an *intelligible* medium.

Commonly, people who think God is the creator of the world have thought that God's creativity is independent of both media. God creates the world ex nihilo – that is, from no material thing which exists prior to God's creation of the world. Thus, God depends on no material medium: he makes the paint and canvas he needs to make his painting, so to speak. Moreover, God himself is sufficiently rich in intelligible content that God gets his very idea of the world he intends to create from no other source but himself. Thus, God depends on no intelligible medium: he does not look abroad, to other worlds or realms or gods, to discover what sorts of things he might make. If this is right, then God indeed is totally, doubly, original: he is the one origin of the material of the world along with the intelligible structure which a material world can exemplify.

## 2 Theory and Worship

### 2.1 God and Abstract Objects

There is a recent body of academic literature in the philosophy of religion which is in the background of some of the reflections offered in this book. This literature concerns what is now referred to as *the problem of God and abstract objects*, and questions whether and how God might be the origin of the whole intelligible medium of creation. The view that there are abstract objects, at least as abstract objects are conventionally understood nowadays,[22] entails that reference to God alone cannot explain why God understands what God understands when he understands how creatures can be. Instead, he gets his ideas of possible creatures by correctly apprehending a realm of intelligibility populated by what were once referred to as 'Platonic Forms', after Plato, and now more often are called 'abstract objects'. These abstract objects are necessarily existent, independent of God, and function in creation as the raw intelligible material of any created thing. The view that there are abstract objects is usually called 'Platonism', but I don't think this is fair to Plato; thus, I use a new term to name the view that there are abstract objects: *abstractionism*; I'll use the term *abstractionist* to describe a person who advocates abstractionism.

The problem of God and abstract objects arises because the abstractionist claim that there are abstract objects seems to conflict with some theological doctrines, in particular divine *sovereignty* and divine *aseity*,

---

[22] Rosen, "Abstract Objects."

the latter so-named from the Latin, *a se*, which means 'by himself'. These doctrines can be formulated in stronger and weaker versions, so we can say that the stronger the doctrine of sovereignty, the more control God has over other things; and the stronger the doctrine of aseity, the less control other things have over God.

If there is, for example, an abstract object which is the property of being God, then God is God just in case he exemplifies this property. But then it looks like God is dependent on a property for being what he is, and this weakens aseity.[23] If God can be God without depending on something else, the doctrine of aseity bids us to hold that in fact he does not depend on anything else for being what he is.

Likewise, if the things which God can create are only things which exemplify properties which themselves exist independent of any thinking or making on God's part, then God's creation of a world is quite a bit like having to furnish a house only with things to be found at Ikea. The celestial Ikea includes all the abstract objects which together constitute the entire inventory available to God for making a world. Insofar as this celestial Ikea is held to exist coeternally with and independent of God, it would seem to compromise God's sovereignty. So if God's creation of a world can be understood in a way which does not make him dependent on the celestial Ikea, the doctrine of sovereignty bids us hold that in fact he depends on no such thing.

The range of views on offer in this literature on the problem of God and abstract objects is fairly represented by the contributions to a recent book,[24] and some of these views pop up in what follows. This Element has some significant overlap with that debate, but my concern is somewhat different.

## 2.2 Creation First

Most importantly, my guiding concern here is the doctrine of creation, not aseity or sovereignty. In this emphasis I take myself to be following the lead not only of Philo himself, but of the patristic and medieval divine ideas theorists who most inspire my own work. For example, consider St. Augustine's (d. 430) influential description of divine ideas. They are the

> original and principal forms of things, i.e., reasons, fixed and unchangeable, which are not themselves formed and, being thus eternal and existing always in the same state, are contained in the Divine Intelligence. And . . . everything which can come into being and pass away and everything which does come into being and pass away is said to be formed in accord with these ideas.[25]

---

[23] Craig, *God Over All*, p. 67.   [24] Gould, *Beyond the Control of God?*
[25] Augustine, *Eighty-Three Different Questions*, q. 46.

The divine ideas for Augustine have a place in theology because of their role in creation,[26] and here are even defined by their role in God's creative activity: they are the unchangeable forms of changeable things – that is, creatures. Similar examples may be found in Pseudo-Dionysius,[27] who probably wrote in the late fifth and early sixth centuries, St. Maximus the Confessor[28] (d. 662), St. Anselm[29] (d. 1109), St. Thomas Aquinas[30] (d. 1274), Bl. John Duns Scotus (d. 1308),[31] and many others.

This Element is therefore more an inquiry into the nature of God's creative thinking than the metaphysics of so-called abstract objects such as properties, propositions, states of affairs, or mathematical objects. The problem of God and abstract objects only arises if we take seriously the sorts of arguments philosophers offer for abstract objects, quite independent of the theological implications of those arguments. It is because the abstractionist's view has a ring of plausibility that religious philosophers have felt the need to problematize it.

But I have next to nothing to say about the independent plausibility of arguments for abstract objects. I am thinking about God before creation, and so thinking of God thinking of creatures before there are any. There is some structural similarity between this picture and the abstractionist's picture: for example, I am happy to say that the Lion, or the property of being leonine, exists independent of all creaturely lions. The abstractionist says this, too. But, of course, I think God is the Lion, whereas they think the place of the Lion is the eternal abstract realm, to which God goes for instruction about leonine nature. So, just to be clear, I am not assuming a broadly Platonic or realist or abstractionistic ontology and then trying to find a way to make it work out with God. I am assuming that God is the creator and exploring what this means.

What I think this means is that God is the sole ultimate source of intelligibility; God himself contains multitudes, more even than Walt Whitman. Whatever exists, whatever can exist, any possible way that things can be, is because God is what God is. God has ideas of all the ways things can be, and he gets all these ideas just by thinking about himself. The exercise of this Element may therefore be thought of as a complement to the Ignatian exhortation to find God in all things. I hope that we will find all things in God.

---

[26] Panchuk, "Created and Uncreated Things," p. 106.
[27] Pseudo-Dionysius, *Divine Names* V, 7, 821B.    [28] Maximus, *Ambigua* 7, p. 99.
[29] Anselm, *Monologion* 9–10, in *Basic Writings*, pp. 17–19.
[30] Aquinas, *Summa theologiae* Ia, q. 15, a. 1.
[31] Scotus, *Reportatio* I, d. 36, p. 1, q. 1–2, n. 69–75.

## 2.3 Rejection of the Gods

This hope that we will find all things in God is the hope both of a metaphysician and of a Christian trying to work out in his sphere of action not only what it means to love the Lord your God with all your heart, soul, mind, and strength, but what it would take for anything to be worthy of such devotion. If abstractionism is true, then I cannot see how God, if there is something deserving of that name or description, is worthy of such devotion.

Socrates – Plato's Socrates, that is – is one unlikely inspiration of this view. Plato's *Euthyphro* ends in frustration. The main characters, Euthyphro and Socrates, cannot together come to a conclusion about the true nature of piety. But while Euthyphro proved himself to be uninterested in dialectic, we readers are invited to pick up where he left off, following the argument wherever it leads. And wherever else it leads, it leads us to the conclusion that the gods of Athens, even if they exist, are not moral exemplars and therefore offer no guidance about the nature of piety and justice.[32] But even if we cannot ourselves claim to know the true nature of piety and justice, we know enough to know that the gods do not deserve our devotion – or, at least, not our unconditional devotion – and this suggests that we have some inkling of something, something which we know is not the same as those gods. Therefore, when the legitimate but conditional claims of the state, or the state gods, came into conflict with the legitimate and unconditional claims of the whatever-it-is which is the source of his knowledge that the gods are not to be in all things admired or followed, Socrates was morally free, even morally bound, to resist – but not harm[33] – the state.[34]

There is some intimation in the *Republic* that this true Source of all righteousness really is one, a unity which contains a multiplicity: the Form of the Good, by which all other Forms are known and from which all other Forms exist. I do not think there is a holier moment in all of Plato than when Socrates asks his fellows to hush before his attempt to descry the Form of the Good.[35] What he was trying to get onto was this One thing which is at the uttermost back of all things, the only thing which could deserve unconditional allegiance, and that's what I'm trying to write about here.

## 2.4 God and Divinity

Those who believe in abstract objects must deny that God is at the uttermost back of things. Ultimate explanation instead taps out at the abstract realm. Of course, even in the abstract realm there will be structure, and an abstractionist

---

[32] Plato, *Euthyphro* 7a–8b.   [33] Plato, *Crito* 49a–e.   [34] Plato, *Apology* 29d.
[35] Plato, *Republic* VI, 509a–c.

might be interested in mapping this structure. One natural aspect of this enter-
prise is to figure out how many *ultimate* abstract objects there are, abstract
objects which explain other abstract objects but which are not explained by any
others. Maybe there are many, maybe there is one. Since I do not believe in such
a realm as the abstract realm, I leave that question for the abstractionists to
answer.

But however many ultimate abstract objects there are, none of them is God.
God, of course, is not an abstract object. God has various features, and so, on the
abstractionist view, he "exemplifies" properties. The properties themselves
which God exemplifies are abstract objects. Maybe there is a conjunction of
properties which God exemplifies, and we can call this big property *the divine
essence*, or *divinity*. On the abstractionist view, if God exists, God "has" or
"exemplifies" or "instantiates" divinity.[36] There are two things here: God, and
the property of divinity. God is God by divinity, or because he exemplifies
divinity. In short, God has an explanation which is something other than
himself. So God is not the ultimate explanation of things. Properties and other
abstract objects are.

## 2.5 The Idolatry of Abstractionism

I think this view is idolatrous, and the way to show that it is idolatrous is
to consider natural, appropriate attitudes which we ought to take toward
ultimate explanations. Consider something, whatever it is, which is the
deepest possible principle of the goodness of all good things. Good things
are great, worthy to be appreciated, admired, and, meeting some high
minimum threshold of goodness, worthy to be venerated or adored.
A very, very, good thing rightly deserves intense admiration or veneration.
But the ultimate principle of goodness, the Good itself, is obviously more
admirable or venerable than anything which is good in a derivative way.
God, on the abstractionist view, is good by Goodness. So Goodness
deserves more veneration than God.

But, "Hear, O Israel: the Lord our God is one Lord; and you shall love The
LORD your God with all your heart and with all your soul and with all your
might" (Deut. 6:4–5). Jewish, Christian, and Islamic worship does not make
sense if it is conditional or half-hearted; it is wrong if the god it picks out as
worthy of unconditional and full-hearted worship is not in fact worthy. So there
is a religious necessity, at least within these traditions, to maintain
a metaphysics which makes sense out of the particular mode of their commit-
ment to their God.

---

[36] Plantinga, *God, Freedom, and Evil*, pp. 102–112.

The theory of divine ideas I defend eliminates abstract objects and holds that God supplies all the ontology needed to explain anything abstract objects explain, and the spirit of the elimination is the spirit of Gideon tearing down the altar of Baal. The fact is that Goodness, Truth, and Beauty, considered as forms or properties which exist in logical space for all eternity, which are the objects of God's knowledge insofar as he has knowledge of Goodness, Truth, and Beauty, and which are the properties God exemplifies insofar as God is Good, True, and Beautiful – these abstract objects, along with the whole pantheon of which they are members, are rivals to God and have no place in a monotheistic system in which the one God is worthy to be loved with all our heart, soul, and might. Tear them down, and say instead that God is the Good, God is the True, God is the Beautiful.

## 2.6 Murphy's Cat

As a matter of methodology, it seems clear to me that Christians should err on the side of having God explain too much rather than too little. As a matter of fact, I think God explains nearly everything, if we are looking for complete explanations. Of course, the articles of the Christian faith do not entail fine-grained theories in every area of human inquiry. There is intellectual work to do which is not the work of theology. But part of what I think it means to be a Christian is to let Christian theology inform as much as possible how we view ourselves and the world. It is a way of life and a worldview, not a theory to be put alongside other theories and evaluated through cost–benefit analysis – though surely God is humble enough to descend even to the level of being one theoretical option among many in the academic literature. Philosophy in particular should be especially susceptible to the allurements of theology, because so much of philosophy tries to uncover the deepest explanations of things. It seems far-fetched, if Christianity is true, that God should turn out to have rather little to do with the deepest explanations of things, and now I think it is time for a story about a cat.

Schrödinger had his poor cat, and there is also Murphy's cat, who, as we will shortly see, is well fed and presumably doing very well. To motivate a view about God's relationship to the moral law which gives God an important explanatory role in the moral law being what it is, Mark Murphy offers us a story about a cat who drinks milk.[37] Suppose you lay out a bowl of milk on your kitchen floor. The next morning you see that the milk is gone. If you are curious you might want to know why the milk is gone. Of course, there are many perfectly logical explanations about why the milk might be gone. Now recall

---

[37] Murphy, *God and Moral Law*, pp. 3–4.

that you have a cat, and your cat drinks milk. This consideration trumps all the others, and makes it wrongheaded for you to go on investigating why the milk is gone. Surely, if you have such a cat, you should just conclude that the cat drank the milk.

Murphy's view is that when it comes to morality, God is the cat. If you believe in God, then it is strange – wrongheaded, even – to go on trying to theorize about the source of moral norms in a way which leaves God out of the picture, just as it would be wrongheaded to leave your cat out of the picture when trying to determine how the milk disappeared. The point here is not just that God is the sort of thing which *could* explain morality and since, gee whiz, you're a Christian and all, you might as well put him front and center in your theorizing. Instead, the point is that God is the sort of thing which obviously *would* have a great deal to do with morality, if he existed. Christianity, along with Judaism and Islam, worships a God who is extremely interested in the morality of his people. The "sacrifice" he desires is a "broken and contrite heart" (Ps. 51:17), and his requirement of us is that we do justice, love mercy, and walk humbly with our God (Mic. 6:8). Jesus's two great commands to his followers are to love God and love one's neighbor as oneself (Matt. 22:37–40). The Beatitudes are far more rigorous and difficult to observe than any regiment of fasting or liturgical celebration (Matt. 5:3–16). Since God is so interested in morality, how strange it would be to let him into your ontology but not into your views about morality, its norms or its foundations.

I think something exactly parallel should inform our philosophical investigations about the ultimate origins of things. The God whom Jews, Christians, and Muslims worship is a God intimately involved in beginnings, the one who spoke all things into existence. His whole case against Job, the case which causes that sympathetic complainer to put his hand over his mouth, is that God alone was there at the foundations of the world (Job 38). He's responsible for the whole show. Of course it does not follow deductively from this that there are not abstract objects which are the eternal properties which constitute God's options for what sort of world he can create. But it is wrongheaded, even to the point of idolatry, to go on asserting the existence of such things if you have let *this* God into your ontology.

## 3 Making Stuff Up

### 3.1 The Aboutness of Divine Ideas

The preceding section motivated taking seriously the theory of divine ideas by showing that it is a metaphysics fit for monotheism: God's own metaphysics, to adapt a recent phrase.[38] Now it is time to get into the weeds and work out, in as fine-grained a way as this short Element permits, a version of the theory of divine ideas which delivers on the promise of a metaphysical theory which is both the sort of theory good enough for monotheism and the sort of theory good enough for metaphysics.

Imagine God at some stage which is logically prior to his creation of anything. So there is God, and no creatures. By hypothesis, there is God and *nothing else*. Even at this stage, God has ideas, at least of himself. But the theory of divine ideas says also that God has ideas of creatures – not actual creatures, since he has not made any yet, so possible creatures. Prior to all creation, God already had in mind all the things he would eventually make, and, plausibly, all the things he could make, even things which he never does make – for example, a real-life unicorn.

So God has ideas of things which do not exist. This demands some explanation. It would be nice to have an explanation of what it might mean for God to have an idea of something which does not exist. It would also be nice to have an explanation of how or why God finds himself stocked with all these, and just these, ideas.

One of the peculiar things about ideas is that they are *of* or *about* other things. This suggests that if someone has an idea of something – let's say, an idea of a dog – then there is something besides the idea, a dog, which is the thing the idea is about. But in the situation we're imagining God in, a situation which is prior to any creation, there are no creatures for his ideas of creatures to be about. There is just God. So what is it that God is thinking about when he is thinking about creatures at this stage prior to there being any creatures?

The abstractionists have their answer ready at hand: God is thinking about the abstract objects which are the eternal archetypes of any possible creature. Thus, when we read in Jeremiah that God knew the prophet prior to forming him in his mother's womb (Jer. 1:5), the abstractionist would say that God knew the abstract object corresponding to Jeremiah – Jeremiah's 'individual essence', as some call it[39] – which the actual man, Jeremiah, would eventually exemplify when he came onto the world scene.

## 3.2 Proto-Creation

If we turn our backs on abstractionism, we need a different answer to the question about the objects of God's ideas of creatures, prior to there being any creatures. Some authors within the classical divine ideas tradition have imagined God performing a sort of proto-creation prior to creation. This proto-

---

[38] Murphy, *God's Own Ethics*, p. 1.  [39] Plantinga, "Actualism and Possible Worlds," p. 111.

creation involves creating something rather similar to the abstractionists' abstract realm. The major difference, of course, is that the abstractionists' abstract realm is totally independent of God, whereas this proto-creation is dependent on God. One proponent of this view, Henry of Ghent (d. 1293), distinguished two kinds of being: *being of essence*, and *being of existence*. God's proto-creation involves the production of beings of essence, and actual creation – the sort of creation we read about in Genesis – involves the production of beings of existence, the former being the exemplars of the latter.[40]

This highly elaborate system seems to have all the advantages that abstractionism has, with the extra advantage of making God the Lord of all realms, even the abstract realm. Like abstractionism, this system says that God's ideas of creatures, prior to creation, are about these abstract objects. Unlike abstractionism, however, this system says that these abstract objects are *created abstract objects*. This is a view defended by some even to this day. In one contemporary view, God creates even the abstract objects which are the properties he himself has![41] In another, God's own properties – the properties God exemplifies – are uncreated, but all other abstract objects are.[42]

Most abstractionists, however, will have no sympathy for this view, because the contemporary conventional understanding of abstract objects holds that these are, by definition, causally unconnected things.[43] That is, abstract objects do not cause anything and nothing causes them. They just exist. It is tempting to retort that this is just a mere metaphysical dogma: there is no principled reason why abstract objects cannot be dependent on something else. In the end I support this retort. However, I do not think you should embrace created abstract objects.

## 3.3 Proto-Proto-Creation

First, there is no good theoretical reason to embrace created abstract objects given the simpler view I develop in this book. I myself do not put much faith in simplicity as an indicator of truth, because I think God may, for fun, make things less simple than they need to be. For contemporary intellectuals simplicity is an important criterion of a good theory, but earlier generations were rather more interested in plenitude: leaving no ontological gaps where gaps can be filled

---

[40] Henry of Ghent, *Summae*, a. 21, q. 2, 4; a. 34, q. 2 (vol. I, f. 124vK, 127rS–vT; f. 212rS); Marrone, "Revisiting," pp. 177–181; Marrone, *Thought of Henry of Ghent*, pp. 112–113.

[41] Morris and Menzel, "Absolute Creation."

[42] Gould and Davis, "Modified Theistic Activism," in Gould, *Beyond the Control of God?* pp. 51–64.

[43] van Inwagen, "God and Other Uncreated Things," pp. 17–19; Rosen, "Abstract Objects," section 3.2.

while preserving coherence and explanatory power. I myself rather like the traditional idea that God has created angelic intelligences infused with distinct areas of expertise and distinct vocations in the management of God's creation – abstract objects reimagined as immensely powerful nondivine persons.[44] Nevertheless, as far as the divine ideas go, they offer a simpler theory than abstractionism, so those moved by simplicity considerations may come to prefer divine ideas on that ground. And it should be emphasized here that the overall cogency of the view about divine ideas I defend does not depend on my personal penchant for plenitude.

Second, and more important, created abstract objects don't provide any real explanation of the original thing to be explained; they just kick the can down the road. To see this, consider that God is an intelligent creator and this means God knows what he is doing when he creates. So God has ideas of creatures prior to making any creatures. But ideas are *about* things, so we're trying to explain what it is these ideas of creatures, prior to there being any creatures, are about. This view, which embraces created abstract objects, says that God creates, or proto-creates, abstract objects, and God's ideas of creatures are about these. But what about this proto-creation? Did God know what he was doing when he made these abstract objects? If he did not, then God makes them irrationally, without knowing what he is doing. But if God is capable of irrational making, then why not just say that God's creation of the real world is an irrational action, something he does without knowing what he is doing? Obviously this won't do.

On the other hand, if God's proto-creation of abstract objects is rational, then we must suppose that he already has something in mind, logically prior to his proto-creation. How did he get these ideas? A proto-proto-creation? But this won't do, either. We would then need to ask whether God's act of proto-proto-creation is rational, and we'd be faced with the same dilemma: either it is irrational after all, and then we have no need to postulate proto-creation of abstract objects in the first place, or it is rational, and then we need to postulate proto-proto-proto-creation to explain how God proto-proto-creates rationally. We'd be well on our way to an infinite regress of proto-creations. Better, then, just to drop the whole idea of a proto-creation of abstract objects, discarding abstract objects altogether, even created abstract objects.

## 3.4 Making Stuff Up

Since proto-creation generates more problems than it solves, you might be attracted to views which let God have all his knowledge of creatures, prior to creation, just

---

[44] Tolkien, "Ainulindalë," in *The Silmarillion*, pp. 13–22; McIntosh, *Flame Imperishable*, pp. 157–202.

by knowing something or other which is internal to himself – ideas only, not abstract objects. In this very broad sense, a theory of divine ideas is just such a theory. But it is distinctive of theories of divine ideas, at least in the classical sense, that God has the ideas he has *because* of what he knows when he knows himself. So the classical divine ideas tradition says that God's ideas are about God. If we say instead, as some modern views say, that God's ideas are not about God, or about anything, but are just made up by God, then we have a view which is like classical divine ideas theories in that it explains God's ideas of creatures without recourse to an abstract realm, but it is unlike classical divine ideas theories in that God's ideas are not derived from, or given by, God's knowledge of himself.

Instead, God just has ideas, either because it is simply a brute fact that God is stocked with the ideas he has, or because God just thinks up his ideas, spontaneously, inexplicably, mentally untethered from anything God knows just by knowing himself. Both of these views, different as they are, are forms of what is sometimes called 'divine conceptualism'. The first view, that God is just brutely stocked with his ideas, I have something to say about in Section 6, "Finding All Things in God." The second view, that God just makes stuff up, I'll say something briefly about here.

The problem is that this makes-stuff-up view makes God irrational. In fact, we get almost exactly the same problem as we had with proto-creation. If God just thinks up his various ideas, then either God had nothing in mind logically prior to thinking these up – in which case he is irrational – or God had something in mind logically prior to thinking these up. But if he already had something in mind, then there is no reason to adopt the makes-stuff-up view. So we have a choice between rejecting this view or embracing an irrational god. I don't see any reason to embrace such a god.

## 3.5 Making God Up

Some have even thought that God makes himself up.[45] But this view, at its extreme, lands us in the nonsense that God, before making himself able to make himself, makes himself.[46] The fact is that in the long history of humans thinking about gods, there are some important witnesses to the extraordinary claim that God is the cause of himself. Ancient Egyptian theology features several accounts of self-generating creator gods, gods who make literally *everything*.[47] And Descartes, famously, claims that God is the cause of himself.[48]

---

[45] McCann, *Creation and Sovereignty*, pp. 231–232; Clouser, *Myth of Religious Neutrality*, p. 361, n. 18.

[46] Bergmann and Brower, "A Theistic Argument Against Platonism," p. 366.

[47] Assmann, *Of God and Gods*, p. 61.

[48] Descartes, "Reply to First Objections," in *Meditations, Objections, and Replies*, pp. 62–63.

I cannot take this view seriously, but I can understand how someone would arrive at this mistake. When we say that God has no cause, among other things we mean that there is nothing besides God which caused God. Attending just to this, we might be tempted then to infer that God is his own cause. But this is a mistake, because in saying that God has no cause, we mean – or should mean – not only that there is nothing besides God which caused God, but that God has no cause.

Now it is natural to seek out what it is about God which bestows on him this power to exist by no cause. When we seek this, we are looking for an explanation. So the correct answer will constitute an explanation of the fact that God has no cause. Whatever this correct answer is, we know already that it cannot be anything outside of God. Thus, either there is no correct answer, or the correct answer is something internal to God. If there is no correct answer, then it follows that God has nothing to do with his existing from no cause. But this sounds very odd. It seems to fail to give God credit where credit is due.

So let's give God credit: God *does* have something to do with his existing from no cause. But then God himself, or something internal to him, constitutes an explanation of the fact that God has no cause. So even if God is not the cause of himself, it does look like he explains himself. And these two concepts, explanation and cause, are closely related and hard to keep distinct. Therefore we should extend understanding to anyone who mistakenly claims that God causes himself.

Rejecting the ancient Egyptian doctrine that God is the cause of himself, let us suppose we say instead, in a spirit of trying to preserve the coherence of the makes-stuff-up view, that God just makes up everything *other than himself*. Then we have an interesting puzzle on our hands. What is, so to speak, on the side of God, such that it is not made up by God? At the extreme, only power is on the side of God, and everything else is on the side of things invented by God. By nature God is powerful, but God is good, wise, loving, and so on because he just made these attributes up and clothed himself in them.[49] Like Craig, who powerfully criticizes just such a view, I do not recognize in such a being anything I am prepared to call God.[50] Being extremely powerful makes God worthy to be worshipped only because that power is wedded to goodness, love, justice, wisdom, etc. *Mere* power – the heat of fire, the force of a wave – inspires fear but is not adorable.

At something less than the extreme, there is at least one thing which God just makes up, totally dissimilar to God. Suppose, for example, that gamboge is a color just thought up by God, answering to no eternal exemplar either in God

---

[49] Clouser, *Myth of Religious Neutrality*, pp. 217–219.  [50] Craig, *God Over All*, pp. 58–60.

himself or in an abstract realm. On this supposition, if God hadn't just made up gamboge, gamboge would not so much have even been a possible color for things to be. I myself find this thought intensely romantic and attractive, and I even (rather modestly) defended it recently, in print.[51]

But the important thing to recognize here is that, romantic as the thought might be of God just thinking up something brand new and utterly unlike anything God already is, such a thinking up would not be something God *does* in any sense of *doing* which is meaningful for distinctively *personal* actions. This is because distinctively personal actions, actions people do *as people*, are intentional actions. And an intentional action is the sort of action a person does when her knowledge of what she is doing partially explains – and so is logically prior to – the fact that she is doing it.

Thinking up gamboge, in the sense under criticism here, couldn't be an intentional action on God's part because prior to thinking up gamboge God couldn't know that his thinking-up activity is the activity of thinking up gamboge. And if not intentional, then God's action wouldn't be a distinctively personal action. It's not clear to me how any action of God's could fail to be distinctively personal. After all, in the circumstances in which we're considering God – that is, logically prior to anything else existing – it is not clear how anything at all would happen were it not for God's intentionally making it happen. But a nonintentional action of thinking up gamboge would have to be the sort of thing that just sort of happens to God, not the sort of thing he sets out to do. So it's not clear what would cause or explain God's thinking up gamboge. If we ask, why was God moved to think up gamboge?, we can't answer that he wanted to, or that omniscience entailed thinking it up, or that the beauty of gamboge compelled him to do it, or that angelic artists implored God to add more colors to the color wheel, or anything like that. God just did it, for no reason and by no cause, nonwillingly, and nonrationally. But I don't see how attributing this sort of making-up power to God is something which accords with any God-honoring religious attitudes, even if it is metaphysically possible that there be such power.

## 3.6 The Biggest Bang

Before utterly rejecting the makes-stuff-up view, however, it is worth considering an *adaptation* of an idea recently propounded by Brian Leftow. I emphasize 'adaptation' because Leftow himself does not think that, strictly speaking, God has ideas of creatures – instead, he thinks that the equivalent of a divine idea of a creature is God's understanding of himself as able to make this or that.[52] But

---

[51] Ward, "Scotism About Possible Natures," p. 398.   [52] Leftow, *God and Necessity*, p. 314.

Leftow does think that God just thinks up the natures of creaturely things, and his view is by far the most attractive and sophisticated defense on offer of the idea that God just makes stuff up. If correct, his view could be adapted for use as a nice way to explain how God could just make stuff up and do so rationally.

Leftow wants to give God a good deal of inventive control over what sorts of creaturely ways of being there are. The nature of water, for example, is, according to Leftow, neither fixed as an eternal occupant of the abstract realm, nor encoded in what it is to be God. Instead, God just thinks up the nature of water. In the Biggest Bang of All, prior to creation, God thinks up all creaturely natures.[53]

Leftow thinks this ideal Big Bang is a rational action on God's part, but correctly recognizes that prior to thinking up creaturely natures, God cannot fully know what he is about to do. He cannot fully know what he is about to do because prior to God's ideal Big Bang, there are no creaturely natures to be known. Thus, for example, when the lion pops out of the Big Bang, God begins to know the lion exactly when it pops out, and not before. If we suppose that, before the ideal Big Bang, God already knew the lion, then the lion would not be among the things which pop out of the Big Bang.

So God cannot *fully* know what he is about to think up, but he can *generically* know what he is about to think up. Consider one of Leftow's helpful analogies. Imagine a very skillful baseball player, who can hit a ball so well that he has control over which direction and how far the ball will travel. Think of the iconic images of Babe Ruth pointing in the direction he is about to hit the ball. But however skilled the batter, he cannot pinpoint the exact region of space the ball will occupy when it lands. Instead, he can determine the general area the ball will land. God's creativity in the Big Bang is a little like this.[54] He cannot know beforehand that a giraffe will pop out of the Big Bang. But he can know beforehand that he is about to think up something or other which has some general features.

Just how specific is God's prior knowledge of what he will think up? As an answer to this question, Leftow reflects on what God would know just by knowing himself.[55] On Leftow's view, God's nature is fixed. God has no say in what it is to be God. So prior to any inventive thinking, God knows himself. Now God, according to Leftow, has the traditional divine attributes: goodness, wisdom, love, power, knowledge, and so on. God is personal. God is a substance. God is powerful. God is creative. And so on – whatever is included in what it is to be God.

---

[53] Leftow, *God and Necessity*, pp. 278–279.   [54] Leftow, *God and Necessity*, p. 459
[55] Leftow, *God and Necessity*, pp. 156–157, 280.

From the fact that God knows everything there is to know about himself, Leftow reasons that God, prior to his ideal Big Bang, could intend to think up natures of things he could cause to exist. He could intend this because by knowing himself he has ideas such as *nature*, *thing*, *existence*, *cause*, and *effect*. Leftow thinks that God can get even more specific than this, but these examples are enough to show the general strategy. Before the lion popped out of the Big Bang, God did not know the lion, but he did know some very general features about himself of which the lion constitutes some specification. He knows he'll hit the ball between the shortstop and the third baseman, but he doesn't know exactly which line it will trace.

Leftow's theory of the ideal Big Bang is motivated primarily by his conviction that there are such things as "secular" natures and "secular" truths – that is, natures and truths which have nothing to do with what God is. The truth, for example, that water has the chemical composition it has is, for Leftow, a purely secular truth. Leftow wants to make all such truths and all secular natures dependent on God's creative thinking, neither fixed eternally in the abstract realm nor encoded into what it is to be God. This is a serious view which deserves careful consideration, and I will have more to say about it in Section 8: "No Secular Truths." For now, however, I want to assert my own view, which is that there are no secular truths or natures. Everything is sacred.

Denying that there are secular truths or natures really just undercuts the motivation to adopt Leftow's elaborate Big Bang. But Leftow's Big Bang is the best thing going for explaining how any sort of making-up could be a rational action on God's part. Thus, as falls the Big Bang so falls the makes-stuff-up view.

## 4 Imitation of God

### 4.1 Divine Self-Knowledge

So, if there is no proto-creation, and no thinking stuff up, and no abstract objects, we need to look elsewhere for an answer to the question we asked earlier: what are God's ideas of creatures about, prior to there being any creatures?

The answer to this question, within the classical divine ideas tradition, is the exemplarist view that God's ideas of creatures are, in some sense or other, ideas of himself. Explaining how this is supposed to work also provides us an answer to the other question we asked earlier: where does God get his ideas? God somehow knows creatures when he knows himself.

### 4.2 Knowledge by Imitation

Somehow. Well, how? We can distinguish two basic views here. One view is that God knows creatures by knowing himself because God's self-knowledge entails knowing all the ways in which God can be *imitated*, and this view is associated primarily with St. Thomas Aquinas and, as far as I can tell, originated with St. Anselm.[56] The other, more traditional, view is that God knows creatures by knowing himself because God himself contains creaturely natures. The first view yields divine ideas of creatures by reflection on the mode of God's knowledge of himself: perfect self-knowledge, which must entail knowledge of how oneself can be imitated. The second view yields divine ideas of creatures by reflection on the object of God's self-knowledge: God himself. I call any version of the first view an *imitative theory of divine ideas*, and any version of the second a *containment theory of divine ideas*. In this section we treat imitative theories; in Section 6, "Finding All Things in God," we consider containment theories.

An imitative theory holds that God gets his ideas of creatures by understanding his own infinite essence as able to be imitated in various, finite ways. God's knowledge of himself as imitable is supposed to follow from God's having perfect self-knowledge, and God's perfect self-knowledge itself follows from God's omniscience, which I gloss here as the attribute according to which God knows everything there is to know. It is plausible to suppose, but it is not obvious, that perfect self-knowledge entails knowledge of all the ways oneself can be imitated.

Plausibly, perfect self-knowledge would entail knowledge of everything that has anything to do with oneself, and imitations of oneself have something to do with oneself. But it is not obvious that perfect self-knowledge entails knowledge of all the ways oneself may be imitated; it is not obvious because an imitation – unless it is an exact duplicate – will have some features which are similar to the thing which it imitates, as well as some features which are dissimilar. It is not clear to me that it follows, just from God's perfect self-knowledge, that he knows all the ways in which imitations of himself are dissimilar to himself. I will offer further reflection on this point later, in criticism of imitative theories of divine ideas. For now, however, assume that perfect self-knowledge does entail knowledge of all the ways oneself can be imitated, and therefore that God's perfect self-knowledge entails knowledge of all the ways God can be imitated.

The great promise of the imitative theory of divine ideas is an explanation of God's knowledge of all the ways of creaturely being, before any creatures exist, merely by knowing himself. The Many proceed from the One as so many little ones. God does not create the world blindly, discovering what sorts of creatures there are only after creating and looking down on the world he has made, as we

---

[56] Anselm, *Monologion* 31, in *Basic Writings*, pp. 40–41.

must look out on the world and have it inform us if we are to have ideas of it.[57] His knowledge of creatures precedes the creation, and knowledge of himself as imitable looks like just what we need to explain this precedence.

## 4.3 Relations and Related Things

Can imitative theories deliver on this promise? I think the answer is fairly decisively "no." There are at least two strong objections to imitative theories of divine ideas. The first comes from John Duns Scotus and will persuade anyone who subscribes to the general principle that the reality of relations depends on the reality of the things which are related. Consider two brothers, James and John. Whatever it is for one thing to have the brotherhood relation to something else, James and John only have brotherhood relations to each other if both men exist and have the same parents. The existence of any two men is of course not sufficient for them to be brothers, since they must also have the same parents, but it is necessary. If their brotherhood is to exist, both men must exist. The existence of the men causes or explains the brother relation, and not the other way around. There might be a very important sense in which John wouldn't be the sort of man he is were it not for his brother James. But we're talking here not of the character or memories of John, but his very existence as the thing he is by nature: a man. Whatever that is, it explains why James has the brother relation to John. In short, relations depend on the things that are related.

Now, imitation is a kind of relation. The statue of Magic Johnson outside the Staples Center in Los Angeles imitates Magic Johnson, and Magic is the model or exemplar of the statue. So, when one thing imitates another we can say that there is both the imitation and the exemplar: the thing which imitates, and the thing which is imitated, respectively.

Notice that if we try to give a detailed explanation of why or how the statue imitates the man, we will point out *nonrelational* features of each. We might say of the statue, speaking loosely, "Look, he's wearing the number thirty-two jersey, and he's extending his left arm commandingly as though he's directing his teammates. That's just like Magic." But these are nonrelational features of the statue. They are nonrelational features of the statue which are also nonrelational features of Magic, or were features of Magic while he played basketball. Crucially, it is because the statue has these (and other) nonrelational features that it really stands in an imitation relation to Magic.

These points about the nature of relations in general and imitation relations in particular are extremely important for understanding Duns Scotus's objection to imitative theories of divine ideas. Here is the objection: the imitative theory

---

[57] Aquinas, *Summa theologiae* Ia, q. 15, a. 2, corp.

holds that God has ideas of creatures by knowing how he can be imitated. But relations depend on the things that are related, and imitation is a relation of a thing to its exemplar. So the imitation relation depends on the thing, and not the other way around. Now God is a perfect knower, so he would know every way in which anything whatsoever imitates him. But, precisely because he is a perfect knower, he would also know whatever nonrelational features of things explain why things imitate God. And even if both the nonrelational features and the imitation relation obtain simultaneously, it is the nonrelational features which explain the imitation, and not the other way around. And God knows this, too. But it follows from all this that God's ideas of creatures are prior to and explanatory of his ideas of creaturely ways of imitating God. So imitation cannot explain how God has the ideas of creatures he has, and therefore imitative theories of divine ideas are false.[58]

## 4.4 Perfect and Imperfect Imitations

There is a second strong objection to imitative theories, which may be helpful for those who for whatever reason reject the principle that related things are prior to their relations. This second objection queries how God, simply by knowing himself, would be able to form ideas of imperfect imitations of himself. In Christian theology, the Son is a perfect imitation or image of the Father (Col. 1:15). But the Son is the image of the Father in the sense that he too is everything there is to being God. The Son is, as we say in the Nicene Creed, "God from God, Light from Light, true God from true God."

There is something ultimately mysterious about how there can be a perfect image in the sense in which the Son is the perfect image of the Father. At the same time, however, it is perhaps more mysterious how there can be, prior to all creation, imperfect images in the sense in which God's ideas of creatures are imperfect imitations of God. To see this, let us think about what it means for something to be an imperfect imitation of its exemplar.

If an imitation really imitates its exemplar, then there is some feature it has which is similar to or the same as some feature the exemplar has. But if it is an imperfect imitation, then either it lacks some feature which the exemplar has, or it has some feature which the exemplar does not have. Consider the statue of Magic Johnson. It has the shape of a muscular man with a ball in his right hand and his left arm outstretched commandingly. Thus far it has features which Magic displayed so many times in his playing days, or at least features very similar to those. But the statue is made of bronze, a quality Magic himself has never had nor will have. And the statue's form of a muscular man is only surface

---

[58] Scotus, *Reportatio* I, d. 36, p. 1, q. 1–2, n. 10–58.

deep; it has no organs and no blood and it cannot sweat. So the statue both has features which Magic does not have, and lacks features which Magic does have.

There is a third way in which an imitation can be imperfect, relative to its exemplar. It might have some feature that the exemplar has, but have it in a lower degree than the exemplar. For example, imitation leather is, let's say, less durable and less supple than genuine leather, and imitation pearls are less iridescent than genuine pearls. This third way of imperfect imitation is very like the first way mentioned above, since it is a way of lacking a feature which the exemplar has. We might say, speaking somewhat artificially, that the genuine pearl has the feature not just of iridescence but high-iridescence, while the imitation pearl has low-iridescence. Then we can express the difference between them either as the difference between having one and the same feature (iridescence) in different degrees (high and low), or as having two different features (high-iridescence and low-iridescence).

So, we return to God and the question of how he might form ideas of imperfect imitations of himself. The claim of imitative theories of divine ideas is that just by knowing himself God knows all the ways in which he can be imperfectly imitated, and thereby has his ideas of creatures. But consider that in order to be an imperfect imitation, the imitator must have some feature which the exemplar lacks, or lack some feature which the exemplar has.

But an imperfect imitation of God could not have some feature which God lacks. To attribute this reality to an imperfect imitation of God would commit you to thinking that there is some reality, some way for things to be, which is not due to God – a view comfortable for abstractionists but alien to divine ideas theorists.

## 4.5 Imitations of Simplicity

So, an imperfect imitation of God must lack some feature which God has. This is indeed a promising route, but it is made complicated by the doctrine of divine simplicity. Traditionally, theologians who have advocated theories of divine ideas have also advocated the doctrine of divine simplicity. This foundational doctrine at its core involves the denial that God has parts. This denial is itself motivated by the nontheological conviction that anything which has parts has some cause – that is, some thing which assembled those parts, thereby causing the thing which is composed of those parts. But God has no cause. So he has no parts.

The denial of composition or complexity in God stands in tension with all the traditional attributes which theologians ascribe to God – for example that God is wise, good, merciful, just, powerful, loving, and so on – to say nothing of the earthier things said of God in the Bible. The tension arises because these various attributes are clearly different from each other. Being powerful is compatible with, but not exactly the same thing as, being wise.

So it seems that, if God really is wise, good, merciful, etc., then he has *more than one feature*: his being wise is not altogether the same as his being good, and these are not altogether the same as his being merciful, etc. But having more than one feature is in tension with not having any parts. Maybe you are not sure whether something which has several features thereby has several parts. Ordinary ways of talking do not offer much help here. But the most influential understanding of divine simplicity involves interpreting "part" in a very broad sense to include not just physical parts like lumber and screws, but anything whatsoever which would entail genuine complexity in a thing. When Aquinas argues for divine simplicity, he denies that God has complexity in any conceivable way in which a thing might really have complexity.[59]

The traditional response to this tension is to draw a distinction between what God is in himself and the manner in which minds like ours access what God is. God, you might say, really is simple *as he is in himself*, but we have no positive insight into what it is for God to be this way. The only way we can access what God is, to the extent we can access it, through a plurality of concepts and terms.

Ultimately, I do not think this traditional response to the tension between divine simplicity and the plurality of divine attributes is adequate. I will explain why in Section 5, "Simple Enough." For now, however, let us suppose for the sake of argument that the doctrine of divine simplicity really does commit us to its strict interpretation – namely, that there is no real complexity of any kind in God. We will see what follows from this.

## 4.6 Degrees of God

It follows from a strict interpretation of the doctrine of divine simplicity that there cannot be imperfect imitations of God, and so God cannot have ideas of creatures by having ideas of imperfect imitations of himself.

To see this, recall that if something is to be an imperfect imitation of God, then it must lack some feature which God has. Lacking some feature which God has could either mean having some lower degree of a feature which God has, or simply lacking some feature which God has. But according to the strict version of the doctrine of divine simplicity, which I here assume for the sake of argument, God has no features. Or, to put it gnomically, God is his only feature. So if it is possible for a thing to imitate God then it looks like it must be a perfect imitation: only something which is what God is will meet the conditions for

---

[59] Aquinas, *Summa theologiae* Ia, q. 3.

imitating God, and this is exactly what Christians believe about the Son's relation to the Father.

Perhaps being God admits of degrees. Then we could say that God, in knowing himself, knows all about being one degree of God, two degrees of God, and so on. Then God's ideas of creatures could be equivalent to his ideas of degrees of God. So a snail maybe is two degrees of God, and a giraffe is nine degrees of God.

This sort of view could get off the ground if there is a permissible way to understand the concept of degrees in such a way that the difference between a high and a low degree of something need not be the difference between having more or less stuff, or more or fewer things. The difference between more and fewer beans is some beans. And the difference between more and less water is some water. But God has no parts such that having more or fewer God-parts would result in a higher or lower degree of being God. And God is not a stuff like water or beef which can come in units like ounces or pounds.

I myself do not see how to make sense of the idea of God coming in degrees which does not result in absurdities like these. But nor do I see how to demonstrate that the concept of degrees couldn't latch on to God in some way which respects what God is and is still an intelligible use of the concept. So to argue against this idea of degrees of God as equivalent to God's ideas of creatures, I will take a different direction.

## 4.7 The Great Chain of Being

This direction involves thinking about the spectacular variety of creaturely differences. Creatures include things like stars and sounds, sand and sofas, starfish and sticky-notes, sepia and succulents, sonograms and sarcophagi. On the old worldview of the Great Chain of Being, all creatures really can be ranked, from smallest to greatest.[60] However, given the spectacular variety of things, it is hard to see how they can be ranked. Ranking seems to require a common measure. Beating all the other football teams makes you first place in football, but it makes you no place at all in chess.

So the Great Chain of Being worldview requires that there is at least one feature which every creature whatsoever has, in virtue of which things may be compared to one another so as to be ranked in one Great Chain. The old doctrine of the Transcendental Properties of Being was therefore a natural ideological companion to the Great Chain of Being. Transcendental properties are those features which transcend or are to be found across all classes and kinds of things.[61] All creatures are *beings* and so they have being in common. But each

---

[60] Lovejoy, *Great Chain of Being*, pp. 58–69; Augustine, *On Free Choice of the Will* III. 5.
[61] Aertsen, *Transcendental Thought*, pp. 13–107.

creature is also *good* and therefore all have goodness in common; is *true* and therefore all have truth in common; *unified* and therefore have unity in common; *beautiful* and therefore have beauty in common. On the old view, these transcendental or most general features of things all admit of degrees. In the case of truth and unity, the contemporary reader might not see right away how these can come in degrees. But few would deny, for example, that a human being is better than one charcoal briquette, or a kingfisher more beautiful than a dollar bill.

So the doctrine of the Transcendentals supplies a way to think about how all creatures, in their wild variety, are relevantly similar to each other so as to be ranked by degree of goodness, truth, beauty, etc.

If we could suddenly see the world again as a Great Chain of Being, each and every thing with its own degree of goodness, truth, and beauty, would we get some insight into how God's ideas of creatures could be equivalent to ideas of degrees of God? Perhaps. After all, classically, God is the Good, the True, the Beautiful. Maybe these features, like all other attributes of God, are in God strictly identical, no difference between them of any sort whatsoever. So if you are willing to say that all creatures have some (degree of) goodness, and if goodness just is the Good which is God, then maybe all creatures have some (degree of) God or divinity.

I will not evaluate this proposal that God or divinity is the one common feature by which all creatures may be ranked relative to each other on a Great Chain of Being. Such a proposal is too wonderful for me.

## 4.8 Spectacular Difference

What I will do, however, is point out that it is one thing for all creatures to have one or more features in common, such that they can be ranked relative to each other insofar as they have varying degrees of their common feature or features, and quite another for all the reality of creatures to be just these common, degreed features. I think giraffes are good and beautiful. And I think lots of other things are too. But I also think giraffes are yellowish with brownish spots, purple-tongued, and adorned with ossicones, which are the things which look like bulbous horns. And I don't think all things are yellow-ish or purple-tongued, etc. More generally, I think that almost every feature which anything can have is a feature which some things have, but other things do not have. I do not claim it must be this way, I claim only that it is in fact this way, in our world. The transcendental properties like goodness, truth, and beauty may well be features that all things have. But even if more properties belong on this list of transcendentals, it is still a short list relative to all the features we find exemplified in our world.

Here is the point. The fact that some creatures have features which other creatures do not have shows that the total reality of creatures cannot be some degree of divinity. It therefore also shows that God's ideas of creatures cannot be ideas of degrees of himself.

What we are trying to explain here is why God has his ideas of creatures. Plausibly there are divine ideas of possible creatures of which we have no notion. But we do have a notion of the creatures of this world, and therefore rightly attribute to God ideas of these creatures. And what we find among these creatures are features possessed by some and not others. Therefore there is more to God's idea of a creature than what it shares with all other creatures. And, therefore, the total reality of a creature is not just a degree of God.

Thinking through what it might mean for God to come in degrees was our last-ditch effort to preserve imitative theories of divine ideas. If God has an idea of how something imitates himself, he must have an idea of that thing so as to be able to see the imitation. This forces us to consider what nonrelational reality there might be in a divine idea of a creature. The imitative spirit bids us say that this nonrelational reality is God himself. But divine simplicity, taken in the very strict sense in which a master like Aquinas takes it, entails that God has no features or has just one. An imperfect imitation of God could therefore only be some finite degree of being God. But this does not adequately explain the enormous diversity of creatures, and hence of God's ideas of creatures. So we must ultimately reject imitative theories of divine ideas, and look elsewhere for the origin of the Many from the One.

## 5 Simple Enough

### 5.1 The Trouble with Simplicity

Does God contain a multitude? The doctrine of divine simplicity as strictly interpreted cries out a loud "no." So it is time to confront this bugaboo head on. We saw in the preceding section that the strict interpretation of divine simplicity caused insuperable problems for imitative theories of divine ideas. At the same time, this strict interpretation is also the very thing which motivates imitative as opposed to containment theories. Let me explain.

Exemplarist theories, like the imitative and containment theories explored in this book, explain God's ideas of creatures through God's self-knowledge. So God has his idea of the lion, and exemplarism says he gets his idea of the lion from himself. The containment version of exemplarism simply says that God gets his idea of the lion by knowing the lion as one of the many which God contains. But if the strict interpretation of divine simplicity is correct, then there is no such thing as a many which God contains. So the exemplarist who adopts this strict interpretation cannot explain God's idea of the lion as God's idea of the aspect of God which is the lion. At best, then, God gets his idea of the lion from his knowledge of himself by knowing himself as *imitable*, lion-wise.

But the imitative take on the exemplarist position breaks down, as we saw in the preceding section. So we have a dilemma: either the exemplarist position is false or the strict interpretation of divine simplicity is false.

The choice is simple: reject the strict interpretation of divine simplicity. Neither faith nor metaphysics requires it. If we reject the strict interpretation, we have no need to revisit the imitative theory and see whether it could be made to work out if the stricture imposed by the strict interpretation of simplicity were lifted. We have no need because, the stricture lifted, we are left with a view of God in which God does indeed contain multitudes. And therefore – so I here assume, and so I argue in the next section – God himself, and not God as imitable, is what God thinks about when God has ideas of creatures.

Now, I take the doctrine of divine simplicity very seriously and I take as nonnegotiable the central convictions about God which are supposed to lead to the strict interpretation of the doctrine. These central convictions are that nothing made God and nothing can destroy God. If we can find some multiplicity in God which does not compromise these central convictions, then we have a view of God which is as good as the strict interpretation of simplicity bids us have, without the problems associated with that strict interpretation.

## 5.2 God Does Not Have an Essence

The guiding light of the exemplarist theory of divine ideas I am defending is that God is totally original: not only does he supply the total material medium which is the created world, but he is the one origin of the entire intelligible medium which comprises all the ways creatures can be. All the real features of things come from what God himself is. When we acknowledge God as the highest good, or the God who is Love, we do not recognize that God himself stands in some metaphysical relation to something else, some abstract goodness or abstract love, and that only by standing in such a relation is it the case that God is good or loving. No, the features God has are features he is, and the features he gives to creatures are too features he is. He in no way functions as a mere demiurge, mediating the abstract and concrete realms. He is the ultimate concrete exemplar of all the ways of being. It follows from this that God does not *have* an essence but just *is* whatever he is. In an old formula, God is identical with his essence.[62]

---

[62] Aquinas, *Summa theologiae* Ia, q. 3, a. 4.

Alvin Plantinga once ridiculed this traditional position.[63] According to Plantinga, the view that God is identical with his essence is ridiculous because it entails that God is a property. According to Plantinga's understanding of properties, a property is an abstract object. So Plantinga thinks that this traditional view that God is identical with his essence entails that God is an abstract object. But God is not an abstract object. Therefore, reasons Plantinga, God is not identical with his essence. Silly Aquinas, for implying something so stupid as that God is an abstract object.

In fact, this is not at all what Aquinas implies. We do not even need to know a lot about Aquinas to see this. Consider the identity claim, that God is his essence. This is a provocative claim, especially if you are used to thinking about essences as abstract objects. Plantinga responds to the provocation by inferring that God is an abstract object and then, because God is obviously not an abstract object, rejecting the identity claim that God is his essence. But he needn't have responded this way. Instead of leaving his contemporary, and therefore somewhat parochial, understanding of essence fixed and subsuming God under it, saddling his opponent with a stupid view, he could have loosened up his understanding of essence and subsumed it under God. In short, with as much logical precision and with far more justice to Aquinas's own view, Plantinga could have said that Aquinas's identity claim entails that the divine essence is a concrete object.

To get a sense of how unfair Plantinga's criticism is, consider a materialist philosopher who asserts that the mind is the brain. Agree or disagree, you know what he is trying to say. But then someone who believes that minds are immaterial souls comes along and says, "Ah, so you think the brain is an immaterial soul. What a stupid view." That is just what Plantinga did to poor Aquinas.

On Plantinga's own view, there is some essence, divinity, and God *exemplifies* divinity. This divine essence which God exemplifies includes the traditional divine attributes, such as goodness, wisdom, and justice. So anything exemplifying divinity will thereby exemplify these other properties – and exemplify them in the highest degree they can be exemplified. God is God, on Plantinga's view, *because* God exemplifies divinity. How did God get so lucky? Well, God had nothing to do with his exemplification of divinity, since he is explanatorily posterior to his essence. God gets to be God because his essence, divinity, is so great that it simply must be exemplified, in any possible world. There is an actual world, which is of course possible (since nothing impossible could ever be actual). So God is here in the actual world. Lucky God!

---

[63] Plantinga, *Does God Have a Nature?*, p. 47.

Now, one strong reason – perhaps the strongest reason – for believers in God to reject abstract objects is that they result in a metaphysical schema like Plantinga's, in which abstract objects and not the living God are the ultimate explanations of what there is and why it is there. Religious devotion should lead us to make God the ultimate explanation. Plantinga's metaphysics makes God a derivative entity – derivative from the abstract essence which he exemplifies. And this is what defenders of divine simplicity care so much about. God is not a derivative entity. So the thing to do is to reduce, or collapse, the whole realm of abstract essences and properties into concrete realities: God and his creatures. This is what Aquinas is up to when he identifies God with his essence.

And Aquinas is not alone. In this respect he's a traditionalist. St. Anselm argues that there is something – the good – through which all good things are good. An abstractionist would say that this good through which all things are good is goodness, an abstract object which is the property which good things exemplify insofar as they are good. But this is not what Anselm means, or says. He uses the concrete form, the good, not the abstract, goodness – *bonum*, not *bonitas*. That all things are good through the good entails, according to Anselm, that the good is supremely, unsurpassably, good.[64] And, of course, he thinks that the highest good, the Good itself, just is God.

So long as we understand the official view, we do not need always to refrain from using abstract forms of words to get onto the concrete ultimate reality which God is. Anselm himself uses both abstract and concrete forms of words to name God, even titling one of his books *On Truth* (*De Veritate*), the whole point of which is to argue that God just is Truth, and the truth of all true things.[65] Also, it is more traditional and euphonious to say that God is Wisdom, rather than the Wise, or that God is Love, rather than the Loving One. It does sound better to say that God is the Beautiful, rather than Beauty, the Merciful rather than Mercy, the Holy One rather than Holiness; but then again Truth strikes me as nicer than the True, and Justice nicer than the Just. But I am no poet, and my efforts here have nothing to do with which forms of words we should use to name God. The point instead is to eliminate any metaphysical gap between property and bearer, predicate and subject, when it comes to God. He does not exemplify anything. He is what he is.

## 5.3 The Unity of God

The denial that God has an essence, or that God is distinct from his essence, is one important part of traditional formulations of the doctrine of divine

---

[64] Anselm, *Monologion* 1, in *Basic Writings*, pp. 7–8.
[65] Anselm, *On Truth* 1, in *Basic Writings*, p. 119.

simplicity. Remember, divine simplicity is meant to safeguard the claim that God has no cause and is dependent on nothing. There is no god which is before God. Nor is there any property or essence before God. God is not good by goodness, he is the good; not wise by wisdom, he is wisdom.

Divine simplicity is also meant to safeguard a closely related claim, which is that nothing can tear God apart. Now God has, or is, various attributes. Even when we understand this claim in the proper way, as not really asserting that God exemplifies anything, we are still left, on the surface anyway, with a multiplicity. So it looks like, in addition to collapsing the distinction between property and bearer, when it comes to God, we also need to collapse all the divine attributes into each other: all these various attributes of which God is the archetype, all these are really just a perfect unity, admitting no distinction on God's part whatsoever.

It is this aspect of the strict interpretation of divine simplicity which must be discarded. But I think I fully understand the motivation for it: if there is real plurality in God, then it sure looks like we can conceive of one "aspect" of God without conceiving of all the "rest." But then there is some sense in which God is separable. Of course, there is no actual power which can break God up, and there is no real worry that God might misstep and break himself up. But the very fact – if it is a fact – of logical separability of one aspect of God from others cries out for an explanation. If, say, we can fully understand one divine attribute without fully understanding all the other divine attributes, then there is no logical necessity which dictates that all these attributes be unified as the one God. But then we could very understandably ask, well, *why* are they together? What is the reason, or cause, of their being unified together in just the way they are unified in God?

And here, to be consistent, we cannot point to anything outside or above God to explain why he is the way he is. But neither can we say that God supplies himself with these attributes. God, we are supposing, is the ultimate reality of any of these attributes. They are nowhere outside of God, unless God makes things which exhibit them. God cannot say to himself, "I would like to become merciful." Snap! "I am now merciful." For God to intend to become merciful is for mercy already to be on the scene as a thing to become. But whence mercy? Not from God, for God thought of mercy prior to his snapping himself into being merciful. Not from creatures, for God could not have made merciful creatures without already knowing about mercy. Not from a realm of abstract objects, for there isn't one. So we must say that God just is merciful, or Mercy. So he cannot *intend to become* merciful.

But again, if mercy, or any logically separable "aspect" of God, can be fully understood without fully understanding all the others, then all these being together in God cries out for explanation. But no explanation can be offered. Therefore, some defenders of divine simplicity opt to take the hard line that God's attributes are utterly altogether the same as each other. In God there is no distinction whatsoever between them.

Now, if we take this route we have to be honest about what we are doing. No one, not even Aquinas, had anything like an insight into what it might mean for all God's attributes to be identical with each other. It is a mysterious view. We back into it, kids groping in the dark, when we come up against the problems associated with assuming complexity in God. But it is a wholly negative doctrine, one more way of saying what God must not be, if he is God.[66]

## 5.4 Formal Distinction

But we need not take this route. There is another way, a secret but not too secret way. Even in Aquinas there lurks the suggestion that not even he really believed in the identification of all divine attributes with each other. He teases us with a sort of distinction which he applies to God, a distinction among the divine attributes which is not due to our thinking of them as diverse but instead due to something about God himself.[67] Whatever this sort of distinction is, it looks to be something more than a mere "distinction of reason" which, in medieval philosophical parlance, is a distinction which is due only to the way that we think about something as distinct in some way, rather than due to some real structure or complexity in the thing we are thinking about.

Duns Scotus developed a similar sort of distinction: the formal distinction. He used it to great effect in formulating a version of the doctrine of divine simplicity which admits some genuine complexity on God's part.

The formal distinction is supposed to be the sort of distinction which obtains in something which is one in number but many in *ratio* or *formalitas*. *Ratio* (pronounced *rah-tee-oh*, not *ray-she-oh*) is a word used to get at the intelligible content of a thing. Words like 'reason', 'notion', 'concept', 'account', 'feature', 'nature', and 'aspect' are all appropriate ways to translate *ratio*. In a real definition of some nature – for example, 'rational animal', which is the definition of 'human' – rational and animal are distinct *rationes* which together make up the one human nature.

*Formalitas* is a word very similar to, if not synonymous with, *ratio*. In the context in which we will deploy the formal distinction – namely, to understand how there can be a plurality in God – *ratio* and *formalitas* are interchangeable. *Formalitas* has no translation to distinguish it from *ratio* in any substantive way.

---

[66] Aquinas, *Summa theologiae* Ia, q. 3.

[67] Aquinas, *Scriptum super Sententiis* I, d. 2, q. 1, a. 2, corp.; Wolter, "The Formal Distinction," pp. 33–35,

For now, I'll use the transliteration 'formality'. *Formalitas* is the abstract construction of the Latin *forma*, which means 'form', and in its most general sense a form of something is whatever is *actual* about it, and in its most ordinary or frequent sense a form is something which actualizes or structures matter or material things. So a man has the form of human, and a red ball has the form of red, and a bronze cube has the form of cube.

The use of the abstract word *formalitas* allows an author to remain neutral about what sorts of actual things, and how many, explain whatever is actual about something. In the examples just used, Aquinas, Scotus, and many other medieval authors would hold that a man has a real thing, a form, as one of his essential or defining parts, and that a red ball has a real thing, a form, as one of its accidental parts. So in these examples the formality of *human* pertains to the man and the formality of *red* pertains to the ball, because of the *form* of human and the *form* of red, respectively.

But something might have, or be characterized by, some formality even where there is no single corresponding form, or even where there is no corresponding form at all. On Scotus's understanding of the human soul, for example, the soul is a form with sensory powers and intellectual powers – it is the form which gives to a human being its powers to sense the world around it and to think. Sensory power is one formality, and intellectual power is another formality, but both of these are contained in, or fully accounted for by, the one form which is the human soul.

God has no forms at all, since a form actualizes or structures matter but God is immaterial. So if there is a plurality of formalities or *rationes* in God, then this plurality is something besides forms. The plurality of divine attributes, in addition to the infinitely many *rationes* of creatures which God understands, demands explanation through some sort of genuine plurality in God. Not plurality of forms, not plurality of gods or god-parts or part-gods, not plurality of bricks or particles, but plurality of formalities or *rationes*. Many of these, but just one God.

So, the promise of the formal distinction is that it gives us a way to recognize genuine plurality in God, such as we need for an exemplarist theory of divine ideas, while preserving the underivative, uncausable, incorruptible unity of God – which is exactly what the doctrine of divine simplicity is meant to preserve.

## 5.5 Divine Infinity

Can the formal distinction deliver on its promise? It can, I think. Formally distinct aspects of a thing obviously imply complexity in the thing of which they are aspects. But these aspects are really identical with God.[68] Hence, these aspects are not like car parts which have to be assembled in order to compose a car and therefore exist prior to being assembled. God's aspects do not exist before God exists, not temporally before and not even logically before. He does not depend on his aspects for his existence, except in the trivial sense that anything depends on what it necessarily is for its existence. (If I were not myself, then I would not exist; but this does not mean that I depend on myself for my existence – except perhaps in a trivial sense of 'depends'.) Whatever structure is in God, therefore, God does not derive from it, but is it – complexity without composition, as some recent commentators put it.[69]

But nothing I have said so far, either about the formal distinction or about God, sheds any light on why God's aspects, considered here either as his attributes or as the *rationes* of creatures which he eternally contains, really are logically inseparable in God. After all, a lion and a lamb are not only logically separable but are really distinct. So why should the aspects of God which are the *ratio* of the lion and the *ratio* of the lamb be logically inseparable? Again, something might have power without having any wisdom: for example, a battery. So why should God's power and God's wisdom run together inseparably?

I think there is a good partial response to these questions, which sheds at least some light. I do not have room to give the full treatment even of the partial response, so I will offer just a bare sketch. The basic strategy is very loosely based on some of Duns Scotus's own reflections about God's infinity – in particular, God's infinity as the key to understanding the unity of his attributes, and God's infinite intellect as the key to understanding God's containment of all creaturely *rationes*.

God is infinite being. His attributes too are infinite. God is good, the Good, good without limit, and therefore infinitely good. And so on for the other attributes. If God did not have each of his attributes in an infinite mode, then there would be some degree of being wise (for example) which God misses out on – there would be more to being wise than the wisdom God has. But then wisdom as such would be what it is independent of what God is. That God is, in the Anselmian sense discussed earlier, the Good itself, Wisdom itself, and so on, entails that God has each of his attributes without any limitation.

But these various attributes, when each is understood to be in God in its infinite mode, seem to be interdependent. For example, there could not be infinite power unless it were wedded to infinite knowledge (for knowledge

---

[68] Blander, "Same as it Never Was," p. 8.
[69] Williams and Steele, "Complexity without Composition."

adds to power), or infinite lovingkindness unless wedded to infinite power (for lovingkindness is a matter of doing and not just intending what is good for another), or infinite goodness unless wedded to infinite lovingkindness (for lovingkindness is an excellence of a person and God is personal so his goodness must involve lovingkindness), and so on. In short, the plausible strategy is to show that for any attribute God has, God enjoys that attribute in its infinite mode, and, moreover, God has one attribute in an infinite mode if and only if he has all his other attributes in their infinite modes.[70]

As for God's containment of creaturely *rationes*, consider that God is infinitely knowledgeable. Even were there no creatures, God would know himself, an infinite object. So God would know his power, and God would therefore know what he could create by his power. There are in fact creatures, so God knows these too. Part of what we seem to come to know by knowing creatures is that things didn't have to be just the way they are; in other words, the world is contingent. God would know the world is contingent, and know all the ways it could have been, or all the ways it could be. But there is no limit to the total number of creatures and possible creatures. God's knowledge contains this infinite multitude, as St. Augustine recognized,[71] about 850 years before Duns Scotus reaffirmed the traditional view.[72] By the way, if there needs to be numbers to count things then God's knowledge contains numbers. But if all you need are things to count, then maybe God is or contains number by his counting, or by the one-to-one correspondence of each aspect of God and that aspect as thought by God.

But why would the omniscient God know this infinity of finite modes just by knowing himself? In short, why is God thus? Here is where explanation comes to an end. I think that God contains these many ways of being, just because. Being divides up the way it does, just because. All the categories, genera, differences, right down to ultimate differences, there is no explanation of why there are just these.[73] Why does animal divide up into species such as lions and horses? Why does one species – say, human – divide up into the very individuals it does? Just because. But there is an explanation of, so to speak, where this diversification takes place, and why the infinite number of finite creaturely ways of being is given, all present and accounted for, prior to and independent of creation, and without need of an abstract realm: the explanation is that this infinite diversity is what God is – but that's for the next part of the story.

---

[70] Scotus, *Ordinatio* I, d. 8, p. 1, q. 4, n. 219–220; Cross, *Duns Scotus on God*, pp. 112–113.
[71] Augustine, *City of God* XI, 10.
[72] Scotus, *Treatise on the First Principle* IV. 48; Cross, *Duns Scotus on God*, pp. 91–93.
[73] LaZella, *Being and Ultimate Difference*, pp. 61–180.

## 6 Finding All Things in God

### 6.1 About Archetypes

The preceding section offered a sketch of an alternative formulation of divine simplicity which left God as intact as even the strictest versions of the simplicity doctrine leave him, but which also left it open that the divine unity embraces a genuine multitude – the Many can come from the One because the Many are in the One. In this section I explore that opening, arguing that God's ideas of creatures are just ideas of aspects or parts of himself.

To begin, it will be helpful to consider one option which so far I haven't considered. I claimed earlier that God's ideas of creatures must be *about* something. The quest to discover *what* exactly they are about has led us to *deny* that God's ideas of creatures, prior to there being any creatures, are about abstract objects or proto-created abstract objects. It has also led us to deny that God's ideas are about God-as-imitable, God insofar as he can be imitated in some imperfect way.

But perhaps the assumption that God's ideas of creatures must be about something is misguided. Perhaps God's ideas of creatures, prior to there being any creatures, are about nothing at all: not about creatures, because there aren't any; not about abstract objects, because there aren't any; not about proto-creatures, because there aren't any. And not about himself, either; not even about himself as imitable. They just aren't about anything.

There is nothing crazy about this. After all, if we think about a divine idea of a creature as the model or exemplar of that creature, then it is easy to think of it, the idea, as that which *other things*, like creatures, are about, but which itself is not about anything. Magic Johnson is the model of his statue and not the other way around, so the statue is of or about him, and he is not of or about it. These seem like very reasonable things to say about how divine ideas would function if they are exemplars or models or archetypes of any creatures, in imitation of which, God might make.

But this proposal has the interesting consequence that God simply finds himself stocked with the ideas he has; there is no explanation for this. Not even God's omniscience would explain this. To see this, suppose that there are abstract objects after all. These things are eternally members of the things which are. Well, then, by virtue of knowing everything knowable, God would know these abstract objects and so have ideas of them.

But on the proposal we are considering – that God's ideas of creatures are about nothing at all – God does not have his ideas of creatures *by* knowing everything knowable. These ideas, on this proposal, are not about anything, so they do not connect God's thinking to anything – until he creates things. They're just pieces of furniture of the divine mind, there forever, inexplicably. Greg Welty has recently defended a view like this. Oddly, he says that divine ideas are uncreated yet dependent on God and distinct from God. So they are neither God nor creatures. They are abstract objects, but they are *in*, not *outside*, the divine mind. Moreover, and most important in the present context, Welty's proposal seeks no explanation of why God has the ideas he has. They're just there, in God, like barnacles on a whale, dependent on God but nondivine.[74]

Now, God is the buck-stops-here explanation of nearly everything explainable. And it is a feature of such an explanation that it does not need explanation. Religious people who look to God as the explanation of things think that things need explanation and that whatever else God is, he does not have whatever features things have that cause them to cry out for explanation, and does have whatever features he needs in order to be the buck-stops-here explanation of things.

For example, according to Aquinas's "First Way," his favorite argument for God's existence, anything which exists and undergoes change cries out for explanation, an explanation of how it undergoes change.[75] Any other thing which itself has just this feature: undergoing change, cannot be the buck-stops-here explanation of how something else undergoes change. The only thing which could be such an explanation is something, the First Mover, which does not have the feature: undergoing change, which needs to be explained, and does have the feature: causing creatures to undergo change, because of which he is able to be the buck-stops-here explanation of the creaturely phenomenon of undergoing change.

These reflections about God and explanation should make it unsurprising that there should turn out to be some features of what or how God eternally is which just are not themselves susceptible of any sort of explanation. Maybe the furniture of God's mind is like this. Maybe there is no explanation why God eternally thinks the (archetypal) lion.

Meaning no impudence, I think we should try to dig a bit deeper. Ultimately, explanation must stop, as I made clear at the end of preceding section, but I do not think it should stop here. I'm not sure that there is anything wrong with letting explanation stop here, other than that I think a good explanation can be given. If one view says that something is inexplicable, and another view says it can be explained, and offers an explanation which really does explain, then that latter view is to be preferred, other things being equal. This is no insult to inexplicable things. If anything, it honors inexplicable things by leaving inexplicability a title bestowed only after great striving on our part.

---

[74] Welty, "Theistic Conceptual Realism," in *Beyond the Control of God?*, p. 81; Anderson and Welty, "Lord of Non-Contradiction," pp. 321–339.

[75] Aquinas, *Summa theologiae* Ia, q. 2, a. 3.

## 6.2 Knowledge by Containment

"Differentiation must come out of the single beginning,"[76] yes, but the best theistic account of how differentiation comes out of the single beginning is that the single beginning is itself an infinite manifold. I think we can offer a good explanation of what God's ideas of creatures are about: they are about God. I will explain what I mean by this claim in this section, but right here just notice that if God's ideas of creatures are about God, then they have some explanation. God knows everything, so he knows himself. If God's idea of himself somehow includes or entails ideas of creatures, then God's ideas of creatures are explained by what God is and by God having perfect knowledge of what he is.

Now God is one, and it might seem to follow from this that when God thinks about himself he has just one idea of himself. But this does not follow. Something which is one may also contain many. This is most clearly seen in the case of things which are made of parts. A car is one car but it contains many car parts. A human is one human but it contains many body parts. A puddle of water is one puddle but it contains many water molecules and many portions of water. In general, if something which is one also contains many, then none of the many which it contains is altogether the same as the one which contains it. An engine is not a car, a heart is not a human, and even a molecule of water or a portion of the puddle, although they are both water, are not altogether the same as the puddle of water.

A master mechanic knows all about cars, in whole and in part. He knows the features of the car as a whole and he knows the features of its parts, how they work and how they work together to make up the one reality which is the car itself. So if God contains a multitude, and if he knows himself perfectly, then God knows himself as one – God – and as many.

Of course, car parts are separable from each other, whereas God's aspects or attributes, if he really has many, are inseparable. But the point of these mundane comparisons of God to creatures is just to crack open the conceptual space to be able to say, intelligibly, that God, by knowing himself perfectly, may have more than one idea: the idea of himself as one, and the ideas of the many which he contains – if he contains many.

## 6.3 Creatures in God

There is something jarring in the thought that God somehow includes all creaturely ways of being. I really am saying that God is the archetypal lion, the archetypal eagle, the archetypal human, and that he is these things because

---

[76] Burkert, *Babylon, Memphis, Persepolis*, p. 62.

there is included in what it is to be God the ultimate reality of being a lion, being an eagle, being a human.

There is a strict parallel here between the traditional attributes of God and these earthy, creaturely attributes of God. Traditional theists are happy to say that God is the Good, or that God is Wisdom, or that God is Love. On nonstrict interpretations of divine simplicity, such as the one offered in the preceding section, we say that while these attributes are inseparably unified in God, they are an ultimate plurality. Because God is Goodness, Love, and Wisdom, any goodness, love, or wisdom we find among creatures has some sort of resemblance to God – God insofar as he is Goodness, Love, and Wisdom. He is exemplary or archetypal Goodness, Wisdom, Love. I affirm this, and likewise I affirm that, because God is the Lion, the Eagle, and the Human, any lion, eagle, or human we find among creatures bears resemblance to God – God insofar as he is the Lion, the Eagle, and the Human.

Containment exemplarism is an alternative to abstract objects, and this is why it is good to use concrete terms to describe the archetypal realities God contains. However, as I said in the preceding section, the theory does not require us to abuse ordinary language. It is fine to say that God contains archetypal *humanity*. What this amounts to is that God contains the archetypal human. As far as the theory is concerned, it is even fine to say that God *is* human, just as it is fine to say that God *is* the Human. The important thing to remember is that insofar as God is human, God is *archetypically* human – there is no property or nature or universal or Form which is God's humanity, the property by which God is human.

## 6.4 Divine Content Duplication

One feature of the containment theory of divine ideas is that it involves content duplication in God. There are all the ways of being, included in what it is to be God. And there are all these ways of being as the objects of God's ideas. In thinking himself, God duplicates himself. What matters here and now is not how this thought might factor into a distinctively Christian philosophical account of God's Trinitarian structure, but rather the difference between God and God-as-thought which is relevant for the doctrine of creation.

The theory of divine ideas is, as noted several times, a traditional way of making sense of God's rationality in creating the world. So when we consider God – God as he is in his essence, to speak loosely – we find there the origin of all the ways of being, hidden away for all eternity. But it is in God's self-thinking that these ways of being are thought by God and so are mobilized for possible deployment in some act of creation. The content is the same – God's

Lion aspect and God's idea of the Lion are duplicates in their content. God doesn't get himself wrong when he thinks about himself. But there must be some difference between them, as there must be some difference between an idea and what it is an idea of. God's idea of the Lion is everything there is to being the Lion plus something like the feature of being about something else. God's Lion aspect is not like this; it is not about the idea of the lion. So even in God there is an exemplar-image structure: the exemplar which is God is imaged in God's perfect thinking about himself.

This exemplar-image structure in God makes some sense of the Christian association of God's Word in particular with creation. If there is content duplication in God, then can't we say that, in Christian terms, God the Father is just as much the archetype of creation as the Word of God? I think the answer to this must be "yes." The Word duplicates the Father, and therefore whatever essential differentiation there is in the Son must track, *ratio* for *ratio*, essential differentiation in the Father. As St. Bonaventure says, the divine ideas which are the exemplars of creatures are not "something distinct from God but are essentially identical with the divine nature."[77] But the Word of God and not the Father has this distinctive note of imaging or imitating the Father, and in this sense the Word, as Word, like creatures, as creatures, has the note of being of the Father, about his Father's business, so to speak.

## 6.5 An Alternative Worth Exploring

You might wonder why the containment theory of divine ideas requires a precise one-to-one correlation between a divine idea and an aspect of God. Wouldn't a simpler alternative – and an alternative which perhaps extended something more robustly creative to God's thinking – be that God can creatively think about the whole reality he is, generating in thought novel combinations or permutations of aspects of God which are given in God's self-knowledge? On this view, we would not have the problems associated with God thinking up totally new content which answers to nothing in what God eternally is. Instead, we would have the same content which God's self-knowledge finds in himself, playfully but systematically reordered in every way in which a perfect mind could reorder it.

I do not see a good way to proceed in evaluating this proposal. My concern has to do with the precise status of these different reorderings of divine content; this is a question about which I suspect people will have different intuitions, and I am in no good place to adjudicate between competing intuitions here.

---

[77] Bonaventure, *Disputed Questions on the Knowledge of Christ*, q. 2.

To keep things as simple as possible, consider a horse and a man and the mythical combination of horse and man, a centaur. Let us suppose that whatever reality or content there is to being a horse and a man are there in God, just by what God is. So God has ideas of horse and man when he has perfect self-knowledge.

Now, at some point or other there is centaur-content in God. Must we locate this content in God, prior to his thinking about himself, or might it be located instead just in God's creative self-thinking, as he combines his ideas of horse and man to yield the idea of the centaur? It is hard to say. If we think of centaur nature as simplistically as possible – that is, as simply the conjunction of horse nature and man nature – then centaur nature is generated purely mathematically, as one of the combinations or combinable things. (It would then be a nonmathematical question whether such a combination is possible – that is, whether there can be creatures which are centaurs in this sense.) It is not clear to me whether this purely mathematical generation should be on the side of God's self-thinking, or on the side of what God's self-thinking is about. I have an intuition toward the latter, but it is a weak intuition.

Still, this crude way of thinking about centaur nature is obviously wrong-headed, since a centaur is not supposed to be fully human and fully horse, and therefore centaur nature would be something other than a matter of being horse and human. What, then? Half horse and half human? *This* half of the horse (legs and body) and *that* half of the human (torso, neck, and head)? If this is all there is, then we still have the purely combinatorial generation of the centaur, in which case, again, it is hard to say whether it should be on the side of God's thinking or what God's thinking is about.

One possibly fruitful complication here is what we might call the *perichoresis* or intermingling of the object and subject of thought in God. God by nature is a self-thinker and God would have reflexive thinking about his own thinking. So a novel combination of divine aspects (just suppose, for convenience's sake, that the centaur is a novel combination) which occurs at the level of his thinking about himself may simultaneously be on the side of what God's thinking is about, since God thinks about his thinking. In the end, perhaps there is not a clear way to distinguish what there is in God just by what he is and what God's thinking generates as he thinks about himself. But I need to leave this as the seed of an alternative worth exploring.

## 6.6 Exemplar Nominalism

If God duplicates himself perfectly in thought, he incompletely replicates himself in creatures. This replication in creatures results in some sort of resemblance to God, a resemblance which must be understood in a way which leaves the distinction between God and creatures crystal clear.

The sort of resemblance we must have in mind here is something like the sort of resemblance associated with nominalism. Peter Van Inwagen has recently described a position somewhat like my own as *divine exemplar nominalism*, and I think it is a fair description, as far as it goes.[78] 'Nominalism' comes from the Latin word for 'name' (*nomen*). It is used to describe a wide variety of views in philosophy, but here is the view which is relevant in the present context: according to nominalism, things which share some feature, for example some humans or some red things, do not literally *share* some *one* feature, say, humanity or redness. Instead, two human beings are similar to each other with respect to those features we associate with being human. Two red things do not share redness in common but rather one is red and the other is red and these two reds are similar. The nominalist therefore takes similarity or resemblance to be rock bottom in the well of explanation of the phenomenon of things sharing features. By contrast, different forms of *realism* hold that similarity or resemblance itself must be explained through sameness or identity. For example, two humans really do share one thing: humanity; and two red balls really do share one thing: redness.

As we will see, the containment exemplarist theory of divine ideas does have some structural features similar to nominalism. With respect to some particular feature of God and some particular feature of a creature, there is exact similarity between God and creatures. But this similarity is not to be taken as implying sameness, as forms of realism would imply. In this sense the similarity between a creaturely feature and some aspect of God follows the nominalist impulse. But this is a delicate issue and much more needs to be said. It may be more trouble than it is worth even to raise the specter of nominalism here, but let me say something briefly about what this containment exemplarism I advocate does, and does not, have to do with the traditional debate about nominalism versus realism.

## 6.7 Universals

Containment exemplarism does not tell us much about what else it might be, in the created world, for two or more creatures to have some feature in common. When we consider the redness of this ball and the redness of that cup and notice that they are named the same, that we apply the same concept to both, we naturally wonder whether they, those rednesses, are really just one thing or are two things after all, despite the fact that we name and think of them as one.

---

[78] van Inwagen, "God and Other Uncreated Things," p. 18.

These phenomena are the data which nominalists and realists explain in their competing ways – and I offer almost no reflection on this debate in this Element. The divine archetype which is the color red, God in his red aspect, is not the very same thing as the redness of the ball or the redness of the cup. Nor can we say that the redness of the cup or ball consists in some sort of relation to the divine red. A color is not a relation. Of course the creaturely redness indeed resembles the divine red, but this resemblance is due to creaturely redness, and cannot be what that creaturely redness is.

But there is no reason to think that this divine exemplar nominalism yields a full-fledged view about universals. I consider this a virtue of the theory: it leaves on the table a variety of views about how to explain this phenomenon of resemblance or similarity between creatures which themselves resemble the same divine archetype.

Maybe God creates red things by creating one single redness which resembles the redness which God is by nature, and this one redness is the one feature which all created red things have in common. St. Maximus seems to have held just such a view,[79] and possibly also St. Gregory of Nyssa (d. *c.*395).[80] Maybe God creates red things by creating this red thing, and that red thing, and so on, without causing there to be any unity, beyond similarity, between the rednesses of each red thing, which is probably Aquinas's view.[81] Aquinas's own metaphysics of universals does not have much at all to do with his theory of divine ideas,[82] but his teacher, St. Albert the Great (d. 1280), identified universal natures with divine ideas,[83] following a not insignificant strand of the tradition.[84] Or perhaps Duns Scotus got it right and God creates individual red things but these all have some unity weaker than identity but greater than similarity.[85] The theory of divine ideas as I understand it does not determine us to any of these or other views. So I want to make clear that I make no claim in this Element about whether some form of nominalism or some form of realism about shareable creaturely features is true.

This is not to say that containment exemplarism does not rule out *any* account of universals. For example, as mentioned, it obviously rules out any view which makes there be something which God and creatures share in common, either in the sense that some feature of God is the one and only reality which creatures have when they have that feature, or in the sense that there is something which is

---

[79] Maximus, *Ambiguum* 7, 16.
[80] Cross, "Gregory of Nyssa on Universals," p. 373; von Balthasar, *Cosmic Liturgy*, pp. 116–117.
[81] Aquinas, *On Being and Essence*, ch. 3, in *Basic Works*, pp. 21–24.
[82] Frost, "Aquinas on Perpetual Truth," pp. 206–208.
[83] Pelletier, "Ockham on Divine Ideas," p. 192.
[84] Klima, "The Medieval Problem of Universals," sec. 1.
[85] Scotus, *Ordinatio* II, d. 3, p. 1, q. 1–6, in Spade, *Five Texts*, pp. 57–113.

neither God nor creatures but is the third feature which explains why God and creatures resemble one another.

Also, it rules out forms of relativism or idealism which make similarity itself some phenomenon which depends wholly on the way in which some individual human being or human community carves up the world. This is because God's nature, reflected in God's thinking, reflected through his thinking and willing into a created world, is the ultimate standard for what things are and so how the world really is to be carved up. If God makes red things, then people are mistaken if they think that there are no red things, or that those things are really brown, or whatever.

## 6.8 Similarity Without Sameness

Leaving aside these different theories about which the containment exemplarist theory of divine ideas claims neutrality, I now want to dig in to what it means for a creature to resemble God.

Consider a particular lion along with God. The lion resembles God. On the theory I am articulating, what this resemblance amounts to is that the lion resembles God because there is a leonine aspect of God. There is much more to God than his leonine aspect, as Aslan makes clear at the end of C. S. Lewis's *The Voyage of the Dawn Treader*.[86] Much more, but no less. God is the Lion. And because God is the Lion, the lion resembles God.

It is also worth pointing out here that there is much more even to the lion than its leonine aspect. For example, it has a determinate height and weight which, we'll suppose, are within the normal range for lions. The fact that the lion is a lion surely partly explains why it has just the height and weight it has. But it does not determine the lion to this very height and weight, and we can see this by reflecting that most other lions do not have exactly this height and weight. So while its leonine aspect surely is the most important thing about the lion, it is not the only thing about the lion.

Now, I want us to focus on just the leonine aspect of God, and just the leonine aspect of the lion. I want to say some things about how this relationship between the leonine aspect of God and the leonine aspect of the lion ought to be understood.

First, God's leonine aspect is the *archetype* or model or original of the lion's. This seems clear enough. Second, the lion's leonine aspect *resembles* God's leonine aspect. This seems clear enough, too. Third, God's leonine aspect *resembles* the lion's.

I think that God's leonine aspect resembles the lion's because I think that in general, resemblance relations are symmetrical: if one thing resembles another,

---

[86] Lewis, *Voyage of the Dawn Treader*, pp. 540–541.

the other resembles it. I think this even in cases in which one of the two things is the archetype or the model of the other. When Omni Amrany and Gary Tillery set out to make a sculpture of Magic Johnson, they knew that their finished product would need to resemble Magic in some important ways – or, at least, ways that are important insofar as Magic Johnson is admired by his fans. If the finished product did not resemble Magic, it would not be a statue of Magic. Another way of stating Amrany and Tillery's task is that they had to give some bronze some features which we can pick out using exactly the same concepts and words we use to pick out some features of Magic. This is just built into what it is to make representational artworks. But if the statue and Magic have features which permit us to use concepts and words which apply equally well both to the statue and to Magic, then, minimally, those features resemble each other, and therefore Magic and the statue resemble each other, even though the former is the model or archetype of the latter. Similarly, God's leonine aspect is the archetype of the lion's. It was God's good pleasure to make a world in which this archetype would be imaged. So his voluntary artistic task was to give some creatures features which resemble his leonine aspect, thereby making creatures which stand in symmetrical resemblance relations to God's leonine aspect and therefore to God himself.

This is a sublime result, and to pull it off without foolishness or blasphemy we must go carefully. The careful way to go is to investigate what this resemblance really consists in. Different answers may be given, and different answers lead us to different theological quagmires. Ultimately, I think we need to say that the symmetrical resemblance of divine and creaturely features really is exact similarity, and that this exact similarity is the best way to understand the traditional claim that creatures *participate* in God. I argue for this claim in the next section.

## 7 The Metaphysics of Participation

### 7.1 Participation by Parthood

Participation is a traditional way of filling out the resemblance relationship of creatures to God which I am here envisioning. Part of the vexation surrounding this concept of participation is due to the fact that in its most ordinary sense, to participate in something means to be a part of it. If you participate in political activism, for example, you do something which constitutes activism: donating money, writing letters, protesting. To participate in a team is to be a teammate, a member of the team. And we can pile on humdrum examples like these.

One of the most august uses to which participation is put, in philosophy, is to explain how something is related to the properties it exemplifies or instantiates.

This use goes back to Plato, who described a thing's relationship to its Forms as participation in them.[87]

The question then arises whether the participation relation, as used to describe the relationship between a thing and its exemplar, is participation in the colloquial sense of being a part of. If we say "yes," then we seem to threaten the sort of relationship which is supposed to obtain between God and creatures, paradigmatically a relationship between a maker and things which are made. In short, participation, in the sense of being a part of something, threatens to *identify* God and creatures.

The most straightforward identification of God and creatures is pantheism, which is the view that everything which exists is God or a part of God. Pantheists would hold that the aspect of God which is leonine is something like all the lions, or the common reality which all lions share just insofar as they are lions. Creatures participate in God, on this pantheistic picture, in the very literal sense that creatures are God's parts.

We cannot consider all the merits and demerits of pantheism here. But it should be obvious that if this world is god then there is no god worthy of unconditional worship. If pantheism is true, there may be a highest object of devotion – Mother Nature – but given her foibles it is unthinkable that our devotion to it should be unconditional.

## 7.2 The Allure of Otherness

Participation by parthood is a way of making sense of the claim that creaturely features exactly resemble aspects of God. It explains this exact similarity through sameness or identity. In its attempt to explain similarity through sameness, this type of participation has one of the same fundamental problems abstractionism has. On the abstractionist view, Wisdom is a property which God exemplifies, and which some creatures also exemplify. It is one and the same property, exemplified by different things. It too therefore explains the similarity between God's wisdom and a wise woman's as sameness; they are similar because they share the same property. In this respect, abstractionism makes God and creatures too close – God is just one thing among many on the dole of the abstract realm. But abstractionism does not make God and creatures as close as does this type of participation, a participation which entails pantheism.

In light of these theological dangers, it might be tempting to give up on the whole idea that creatures exactly resemble God. Maybe we should say something more like this: features that ordinary religious talk appears to attribute both to God and to creatures are not in fact exactly the same features, or exactly

---

[87] Plato, *Phaedo* 100d.

similar features. For example, we say things like, "God is wise, and Socrates is wise," "My mom is loving, and God is loving," and lots of others like these. But maybe the features which God and creatures seem to have in common are, in reality, a little bit like but a little bit unlike each other, and the participation of creatures in God really just amounts to this partial resemblance of creatures to God.

## 7.3 Not Wholly Other

Suppose you say, God's lovingkindness is a little bit like, and a little bit unlike, my mom's. What could account for this? Borrowing from Aquinas, we might distinguish between the perfection itself that lovingkindness is, and the mode in which any loving thing is related to lovingkindness.[88] In the case of my mom, she has lovingkindness as a feature, and a feature she need not have to be the very substance she is. But in the case of God, God is Love, so God's lovingkindness is not a feature he has but the very substance he is. Still, despite these different modes of relating to lovingkindness – having it in the case of my mom, being it in the case of God – we can attend to the perfection itself that lovingkindness is, and ask how God's is related to my mom's. If we assume that, with respect to this very perfection, God's lovingkindness is a little bit like and a little bit unlike my mom's, then it follows that loving-kindness is a feature which has some sort of complexity, some parts or degrees which God's lovingkindness shares with my mom's, in virtue of which they are "a little bit like," and some other parts or degrees in virtue of which they are "a little bit unlike."

But we cannot explain the difference between God's lovingkindness and my mom's by appeal to different parts of lovingkindness. This is because loving-kindness needs all its parts to be lovingkindness. Suppose lovingkindness is the quality of being loving, and suppose being loving is the quality of willing another person's good for his own sake and not for your own advantage. Now we have a definition of lovingkindness. But if we take any of the parts of the definition away, we lose lovingkindness.

It does seem like lovingkindness comes in degrees. It is not hard at all to conceive one person as being *more* loving than another, where we do not mean to say that that other person is not loving. He too is loving, just not as loving as the first. So maybe the difference between God's lovingkindness and my mom's is to be found in the degree of lovingkindness in each. My mom's – meaning no disrespect – is finite, whereas God's is infinite. There is no limit to his loving-kindness. So maybe we can say that my mom's lovingkindness really is a little

---

[88] Aquinas, *Summa theologiae* Ia, q. 13, a. 3, corp.

like and a little unlike God's lovingkindness: it really is lovingkindness, but it is a finite degree of lovingkindness.

Unfortunately, attractive as this picture is, it will not do. This is because what we are saying is that my mom has lovingkindness, and God is lovingkindness, and because he just is lovingkindness his lovingkindness is without limit. As far as lovingkindness itself goes, it is the same for my mom and for God – it's lovingkindness she has and lovingkindness he is – and what my mom lacks is not lovingkindness but infinite lovingkindness. But, whether finite or infinite, lovingkindness is lovingkindness. So what is different here is not my mom's and God's lovingkindness; what is different is instead the degree to which each has lovingkindness. So what we really need to say are a little like, and a little unlike, each other, is God's infinite lovingkindness, and my mom's finite lovingkindness. These two things, infinite lovingkindness and finite lovingkindness, are indeed a little like, and a little unlike, each other.

We then seem forced to say that if God and creatures are similar to each other with respect to some feature, even some feature like lovingkindness which can come in degrees, then they are *exactly similar* to each other with respect to that feature. And our attempts so far to say what this similarity might be, some form of sameness which pushes us toward either pantheism or abstractionism, are not very promising.

Why not then just reject similarity altogether? Maybe after all we should embrace an unapologetic, unrelenting doctrine of God's transcendence. On this view God is totally unlike creatures. He has nothing in common with them. God and creatures are not similar to each other. God is, as is sometimes said, *wholly other*. Here's the picture: my mom's lovingkindness is not like God's. His is wholly other from hers.

## 7.4 Wholly Other

This is a severe doctrine. Let us make sure we are clear-eyed about what it involves. Among several lines we might pursue, I want to tease out what this wholly other doctrine means for creation and God's creativity. Consider one of our foundational commitments: that God knows what he is doing when he creates. He knows what he is creating. God's knowing is logically prior to his making: he knows what he makes before he makes it. So his knowledge of creatures is not dependent on there being any creatures. Now consider one of our foundational questions: why does God have the ideas he has? The view for which I have argued is that he has these ideas because he knows himself perfectly. God knows creatures by knowing himself.

But if God is wholly other than creatures, then God cannot know creatures in advance of creation by knowing himself. This is because, on the wholly other doctrine, God is wholly unlike creatures. So there is nothing about God which, in knowing himself, will yield to himself any notion of a creature.

Where, then, will the proponent of the wholly other view turn? How does God know creatures in advance of his making any? I think there are exactly three options: first, he just invents them, whole cloth, utterly from nothing. Second, he looks outside himself, to a realm of coeternal principles, perhaps abstract objects, and in knowing them knows creatures in advance of creation. Third, he does not know creatures before making them. He just makes them, and then, so to speak, discovers what he has made.

The problems with the first view were discussed in Section 3: "Making Stuff Up." The problems with the second view were addressed in Section 2: "Theory and Worship." The problem with the third view is that it makes God an irrational creator, indeed, no longer deserving of the title 'creator' at all.

William of Ockham (d. 1347) arrived at the brink of the abyss which is this third view – and dived right in. He was paying mere lip service to St. Augustine and the divine ideas tradition when he wrote that a divine idea of a creature just is the creature itself.[89] He could not draw up from the well of divine simplicity – as he understood it, like Aquinas, in the strict sense – anything like a creature, and so could find no holding place in God's mind, in advance of creation, for ideas of creatures.[90] Prior to creation, creatures are nothing at all: not creatures, not proto-creatures, and not even twinkles in God's eye – just nothing at all.[91] The divine idea of a creature is the creature, and so there is no such thing as a divine idea of a creature independent of or prior to a creature. Of course, prior to creation, God can produce creatures because he is omnipotent and knows himself as omnipotent, and in this attenuated sense God may be said to know creatures before creating them. But even once there are creatures, God's idea of a creature is the creature insofar as it is something producible by God.[92] When we recall that, according to Ockham, what is producible by God is everything whatsoever which is not logically contradictory, it follows that what God knows when he has a "divine idea" of a creature is his own omnipotence. All the spectacular variety of things, all the joy and all the suffering – Ockham's God has no notion of any of this. He is locked in his own head, eternally contemplating power.

---

[89] Ockham, *Ordinatio* I, d. 35, q. 5, p. 488, l. 15.
[90] Klocker, "Ockham and the Divine Ideas," p. 357.
[91] Ockham, *Ordinatio* I, d. 36, q. 1, p. 547, ll. 11–19; Pelletier, "Ockham on Divine Ideas," pp. 208–209.
[92] Ockham, *Ordinatio* I, d. 35, q. 5, p. 486, ll. 2–4.

Still, so vexed might you be by the problems associated with affirming real resemblance between God and creatures that you might not mind embracing one of these other three alternatives, even the third, Ockhamist alternative, however bleak they seem. But I have good news for you. There is a very respectable understanding of participation in the offing, one which solves our problems.

## 7.5 Participation Vindicated

We do not need to go down the dark and lonely path of nonparticipation. God is here with us, and God is like us, and because he is like us he can form rational plans about a world he wants to make, and then make it. All of this is worth holding onto. In the end I do think there is a perfectly decent account of participation. I think all there is to the participation of creatures in God is resemblance to God, a resemblance which, at the level of discrete aspects of God and discrete aspects of creatures, is exact similarity. This is all there is to participation,[93] but this is quite a lot!

Creatures resemble God, as statue to model, image to archetype. In creation, what God gives is not himself but a new thing: creatures that exist and whose existence is not God's existence. God does not give exactly himself, but what he gives is exactly like some aspects of himself. This goes for creaturely lovingkindness, creaturely lion, and even creaturely being itself. Yes, a creature's being is exactly like God's being, attending precisely to being. Of course, God is infinite being, and any creature and any collection of creatures is just finite being. But, like the lovingkindness of my mom, which is exactly like God's lovingkindness even though his is infinite and my mom's is finite, even though hers is an image and God's the archetype, the being of a creature is exactly like God's being, even though his is infinite, and his the archetype.

And this, by the way, is nothing more and nothing less than Scotus's doctrine of the univocity of being, the doctrine that we can correctly conceive both God and creatures under one concept,[94] univocally. The doctrine of the univocity of being does not imply some third thing, being, which God and creatures share. Nor does it imply that the being of God is the very being which is the being of creatures, numerically identical with it. No, the doctrine of univocity simply means that a creature's being, just insofar as it is being, is exactly like God's. Therefore we can have just one concept which applies to both. Univocity is in fact the only doctrine which explains the participation of creatures in God in

---

[93] Bonaventure, *Disputed Questions on the Knowledge of Christ*, q. 2.
[94] Scotus, *Ordinatio* I, d. 3, q. 1, in *Philosophical Writings*, pp. 13–33.

a way that avoids pantheism or abstractionism. What Scotus has sometimes been accused of destroying,[95] he in fact vindicates.

Creation really is creation. It really is out of nothing. The central mystery of the metaphysics of God's creation of a world is that there should be something besides himself. That there can be something besides God is, perhaps, evident from our experience of things. How there can be something besides God is utterly mysterious. Of course we appeal to divine power, God's total power. As Aquinas says, omnipotence takes into its scope the whole of producible being. So an omnipotent God is able to make all makeable things, matter and form.[96]

We ourselves make by pushing, pulling, tearing, joining, lifting, placing, speaking, writing, and we do all these things to other things. But whatever action it is by which God creates the whole of creaturely being, it is an action beyond even the analogical imagination. We can indeed think through, a bit, how God might have ideas of creatures through knowing himself, and how God's rationality and freedom might be involved in the selection, from among countless possibilities, of this world. And from here we can inch toward assigning some meaning to the thought that God has creatures in mind when he makes the world. But what the action of divine making itself is, in isolation from whatever is in God's mind when he makes, of that we have no ken.

And here is the leap of faith for those who believe that the world is a created thing: to believe that the world really is something besides God, for all its similarity to God. It is after all easier to understand creation merely as God's thinking. All of this, all around us, is going on in God's mind – nowhere else! On this idealist view there is perhaps no distinction at all between the real world and any number of possible worlds with their possible histories which play out in God. Maybe we could distinguish the real world as the world which is God's favorite, or something like that, and imagine him giving it more attention than all the others. But we would relieve ourselves of the problematic mystery at the core of the doctrine of creation: that God managed to make something.

I think we need to hold onto this idea that creation really is something new. That God thought the world worth making, when he didn't need to make it, is a thought which is encouraging to me and keeps me on the hunt for the life I know I am supposed to live. I do not like the thought of being only something God is dreaming. I like much better the thought that I approach my best life by approaching God's dream of me – or, as St. Maximus says, by approaching the little logos which is that part of the divine Logos which is God's paradigm of

---

[95] Pickstock, "Duns Scotus," p. 550.   [96] Aquinas, *Summa theologiae* Ia, q. 45, a. 2–4.

me[97] – and that of course requires a distinction between God's dream and the waking world, between paradigmatic logos and imaging logos.

So while it is a leap of faith for the believer in creation to hold onto the view that God really has made something new in making the world – not to mention the remaking of the world which we resurrectionists also think he will do – it is a leap worth taking. Not pantheism, not abstractionism, not indiscriminate blasts of divine power, not idealism: creation. Creation, and so participation by resemblance.

## 8 No Secular Truths

## 8.1 The Ultimate "Why" Question

That there is something rather than nothing is an interesting fact, but it is not nearly so interesting as the fact that things are *such* as they are. It strikes us that things needn't have been just as they are. To some, myself among them, our experience of our own freedom makes it self-evident that we have free will,[98] and therefore that things in general can be otherwise. So why are things just this way? One sort of answer is that history has gone a certain way: long ago, this happened, then that, and the other, and so on, and this explains why things are (now) the way they are. The theistic claim is of course that God has something to do with history itself being a certain way. So God must have something to do with why things not only are, but are such as they are.

There are some voices in the tradition which insist that God must have created, that it is inconsistent with his goodness or whatever to refrain from creating.[99] I do not have space to respond to those voices here, though I disagree with them. Other voices, however, insist not so much on God's freedom or unfreedom to create at all, but rather on God's unfreedom about what gets created. Some have thought that there is such a thing as the best way for creation to be, and that it follows from God's infinite goodness that if he creates, he creates the best.[100] Others, at least some Christian Neoplatonists, have thought that if God creates, he creates everything he could create, leaving nothing in reserve.[101]

These problematic views fail to appreciate God's freedom and God's infinity. If God is infinitely good, then he is not better off by creating rather than refraining from creating. Creation, like salvation, is God's free gift. And if any possible created order is only finitely good, then there is no such thing as

---

[97] Maximus, *Ambiguum* 7, 17.   [98] Reid, *Essays on the Active Powers of Man* IV, ch. 2.

[99] Bonaventure, *Sent.* I, d. 45, q. 1; Avicenna, *Metaphysics* IX, ch. 1, par. 2.

[100] Leibniz, *Discourse on Metaphysics* 3.   [101] Gersh, *From Iamblichus to Eriugena*, p. 138.

a best possible world: for any world, there is a better.[102] What God creates, then, really is up to God.

Some might say that God's options are constrained by some minimal threshold of goodness in the worlds which are his options. A very bad world, for example, just would not be on the table for God. My own take on this suggestion is that if God is what we should think he is, there are no such things as bad worlds. If you are trying to imagine a world created by God which, let us say, features intensely degrading suffering of all sentient creatures with no redemption, then you are trying to imagine a square circle. Such a world, created by God, is not logically possible. And if you think, as you should, that it is not logically possible that there should be a world which is not created by God, then there is no such thing at all, anywhere, not in God or God's thoughts or the abstract realm, as such a miserable world. God does not so much even think such a world, for there is nothing to think about – though, of course, he would know all about our philosophical attempts to employ such a world in philosophical reasoning about the problem of evil, knowing all there is to know about being mistaken in thinking such a world is logically possible. So God's real options for worlds he might make are all good, because they are all worlds which, if they should exist, would be made by a God who is infinitely good.

If there is no such thing as a best world, and if among worlds there are only such things as good ones, then we must imagine God's freedom in creating as simply picking, as Al-Ghazali's (d. 1111) man just picks one of the dates before him.[103] But despite this emphasis on God's freedom in choosing which world to make, if any, we must also resist the impulse to answer our ultimate why question by leaving *everything* to God's will. Austen Farrer foundered on just this point, so fascinated was he by the contingency of creation that he could only ascribe the way things happen to be to God the Unconditioned Will.[104] The problem here is lack of attention to divine psychology in creating. God's creativity is logically prior to his creating, and his creativity means – if we mean anything at all when we say that God is the person who created the world – that he knows what he is doing when he creates. God has options, and therefore his creation is not the product of Unconditioned Willing. It is instead the product of a willing which is conditioned by what God himself is. God contains all the genuinely possible worlds, and these are his options. He gives in creation only of what he already is. But what he is is so bountiful that he can create the unfathomable stars and the people who can contemplate them, and leave infinitude in reserve.

---

[102] Aquinas, *Sent.* I, d. 44, q. 1, a. 2; Kretzmann, *The Metaphysics of Creation*, pp. 216–227.
[103] Al-Ghazali, *Incoherence*, Prob. 1, pp. 26–27.
[104] Farrer, *Faith and Speculation*, pp. 112–118.

## 8.2 No Authorless Books

These reflections on worlds God might create invite some additional reflection on God's relation to possible worlds. God is the archetype of all creatures. A merely possible creature is a creature God could make but has not. We can talk about groups of possible creatures, even very large groups of possible creatures, all the way up to whole worlds of possible creatures. A world extremely different from this world is possible, let's suppose, and so it, taken as a whole, is a really big possible creature – that is, a thing God could make. This, I suggest, is a natural way to look at the nature of possible worlds on a traditional theory of divine ideas.

What I am calling a natural way to think about possibility on the divine ideas theory is in fact rather puzzling from the standpoint of mainstream contemporary metaphysics. On the mainstream view, initiated by Saul Kripke in the late 1950s[105] and developed into a full-blown metaphysics by 1970,[106] to be possible is to exist in at least one possible world. To be actual is to exist in the actual world. To be contingent is to exist at least in the actual world, perhaps also in other possible worlds, but not in all possible worlds. To be necessary is to exist in all possible worlds, and to be impossible is to exist in no possible worlds. It is hard to overstate the importance of this "possible worlds" framework for contemporary philosophy of language, metaphysics, and philosophy of religion, in addition to other subfields of philosophy. The most famous application of this framework in the philosophy of religion is Alvin Plantinga's possible worlds argument for God's existence.[107] At least for this reason, but probably for others, the possible worlds framework has long been considered a friend of theistic philosophy of religion.

On Plantinga's view, possible worlds are very complex abstract objects.[108] After asking an audience in 1980 whether God might have something to do with the existence of abstract objects,[109] Plantinga answered his own question in the affirmative just two years later, embracing something like a theory of divine ideas.[110] But while he has kept on embracing it,[111] to date he has not worked out a nuanced version of the theory. Nor has he published anything which indicates recognition of the deep tension between the divine ideas theory and the possible worlds approach to the metaphysics of possibility and necessity.

---

[105] Kripke, "A Completeness Theorem," pp. 2–3.
[106] Kripke, *Naming and Necessity* (published in 1980 but first given as lectures in 1970).
[107] Plantinga, *God, Freedom, and Evil*, pp. 85–112.
[108] Plantinga, *Nature of Necessity*, pp. 44–46.
[109] Plantinga, *Does God Have a Nature?*, pp. 145–146.
[110] Plantinga, "How to be an Anti-Realist," pp. 69–70.
[111] Plantinga, *Warrant and Proper Function*, pp. 121; *Where the Conflict Really Lies*, p. 291. Both cited in Craig, *God Over All*, p. 73.

Broadly speaking, in the divine ideas tradition, God exists necessarily, and everything else which exists does so contingently. An emphasis on God's freedom leads most in this tradition to hold that God could have made things different from the way things are, and might not have made anything at all. Fitting this vision into the possible worlds framework is a lot like trying to shove the glass slipper on one of the wicked stepsisters' feet: maybe you can ram the slipper on, but it's not a good fit.

Consider: on the possible worlds framework, to be necessary just is to exist in all possible worlds. Thus, God's necessity is, within this framework, interpreted as God's existence in all possible worlds. But within the divine ideas tradition, it is more natural to think of a possible world as a world God can make. But God cannot make himself. So God cannot be in a possible world. But by this conclusion the divine ideas theorist such as myself does not mean to talk like the possible worlds theorists talk, for in their language "God exists in no possible world" just means "God cannot exist." But the divine ideas theorist doesn't mean this. Quite the contrary! In saying that God exists before all worlds, the sole source of their intelligible content, holding them all before his mind as so many ideas, the divine ideas theorist emphatically affirms that God exists.

We could hold out hope for some successful translation work between these two views of possible worlds, as we might hold out hope that a long and painful foot-binding regiment might let the slipper slip on. To begin, we'd need to make some distinctions and standardize terminology, starting with 'world'. Part of what the divine ideas theorist means by 'world' is a thing that God can make, as when we say in Sunday School that God's got the whole world in his hands. The actual world is all God has made: a total creaturely story. A merely possible world is a different total creaturely story God could have told, as a possible tale of Middle Earth is a tale Tolkien could have written. The author of a story has a whole lot to do with the story he writes, but the author is no part of the thing made; the author does not make himself. But this is not what 'world' means for the possible worlds theorists. They mean something more like Wittgenstein's definition of world: the world is everything that is the case.[112] Since it is the case that God exists, God is in the actual world. And if it turns out, as Plantinga's famous argument tries to show, that there is no possible world in which it is not the case that God exists, then God is in every possible world.

The problem is that on Plantinga's view, each book or story of a possible world is a book no one has written, not even God. Even worse, God is but a character in these books of worlds. Yes, his exemplification of the property of

---

[112] Wittgenstein, *Tractatus Logico-Philosophicus* 1.

maximal greatness entails that he is the most important character in each book, and even that he has read all the books. But he wrote none of them. No one wrote them. The books are brute facts, dependent on God neither for their existence nor their content.

Plantinga's system also entails that God has nothing to do with which world is actual. We cannot say that this actual world is the world God has made because God himself is part of the world and God can't make himself. Nor can we say that God caused there to be this world rather than some other world, for God can't do anything unless he is actual, and he is actual only because he is an inhabitant of the actual world.

Is there some reason why the book of this world was selected to be read, rather than some other book? Who knows? More disconcertingly, is there any assurance that this book continues to unfold? What makes it impossible, if it is impossible, that this unfolding story just breaks off, gets put back on the shelf, and another one gets started? What if Fate is a fickle dilettante, never finishing a book? If there is assurance to be had here, God does not provide it.

The alternative divine ideas picture is something very different: there are no worlds, no abstract objects at all. Their closest analogues are all in God. God is the exemplar of all the ways of being – the true philosopher's paradise is God himself, *pace* David Lewis.[113] Without God there is nothing at all. If there is anything besides God it is because of God. God by nature is not caused to exist by anything and is not sustained in existence by anything. As the all-powerful, rational God he creates, if he creates at all, in an orderly and good way, beholding in thought all possible creaturely stories. He creates, if he creates, by selecting one of these stories, freely, without compulsion. The total creaturely story of course includes God as the heroic main character. But author and character are one.

## 8.3 Evil as Privation

Should we expect a better world from such an author? Sometimes I think so. But I do not ask the question to begin any sort of attempt to justify the ways of God to men insofar as those ways include the permission of horrific evils. Instead, I want to focus on a potential objection to the containment exemplarist view which I have developed in this book, an objection which would run something like this: if every creaturely reality has its exactly similar exemplar in God, then God is evil, or at least contains evil. This is because some creaturely realities are evil. But no being worthy to be worshipped as God is or contains evil.

---

[113] Lewis, *On the Plurality of Worlds*. I owe this favorable comparison of my view to Lewis's to an anonymous referee.

I take the objection seriously, and I cannot exhaustively defend my view against it here. But my basic response is to embrace the old metaphysics of evil as the mere privation of good, and I think this makes a good start toward a successful response to the objection. I do not think there are any real evils. Sixteen hundred years after Augustine, I repeat what he said: God did not create evil, because evil is not a thing to be created.[114] And I add that because evil is not a thing to be created, God does not contain evil in any sense inconsistent with the sort of unconditional worship we owe him.

Of course God contains evil in other senses. Consider a faithful priest who hears many confessions. Whatever evil he did not know from his own sinfulness, he knows, in abundance, from hearing the confessions of many sinners. But all the sinful content which goes into the mind of the priest does not defile him, even if, given the priest's own sinfulness, he could defile himself with the knowledge he receives in the confessional. But by the same token, his expansive knowledge of evil could help him counsel other sinners better than he might otherwise have been able to.

If a priest, in principle, could hear all the sins of the whole world and be the better for it, how much more so can God? God's will is perfect, so in knowing all the ways in which creatures can go wrong, he is not tempted to sin. And of course we ought to attribute to God the most disgusting, the most absurd, the most malicious of all thoughts. God is not some Ned Flanders churchman whose sanctity depends on shielding himself from bad thoughts. God has all these base thoughts, but he does not entertain these thoughts in a way which impugns his goodness.

Also, we must remember that things which for us are repugnant or gross probably are not so for God. I'm not only a little scared of cockroaches, I'm disgusted by them, associating them as I do with filth and decay, and therefore with sickness and death. But God is neither scared nor disgusted by cockroaches and other repugnant things.

So imagine God with his idea of our world, logically prior to creating it. As I have argued, he has his idea of this world by knowing that aspect of himself which is the exemplar of this world. When he sees all the things wrong with the world, does he thereby see what is wrong with himself? I don't think so, because, again, I think that, strictly speaking, what is wrong with the world is what God does not see in it – not because God has poor vision but because some good is not there to be seen. And a privation of a good thing, while bad, is no thing of which there can be an exemplar in God. Bad as our world is, we must not forget either its great goodness – *Robinson Crusoe* is helpful on this point – or the fact that any

---
[114] Augustine, *Confessions* VII. xi–xiii.

world, from God's perspective, will have a great deal of good which God does not see there.

## 8.4 No Secular Truths

That there is no substance to evil, in the deepest heart of being, is a rather extreme corollary of a weaker thesis, which is that everything is sacred: there are no merely secular truths. The sense of "secular truth" I have in mind here is a semi-technical sense which comes from Brian Leftow's monumental book, *God and Necessity*. Consider a necessary truth about something which does not seem to have anything to do with God: water is $H_2O$. Leftow wants to make this and every other secular truth dependent as much as possible on God's contingent, creative thinking.

Leftow's motivation is pious. He wishes to preserve what he calls 'divine ultimacy' – God's being the sole ultimate reality.[115] I share this pious motivation, and it has led me to the containment exemplarist view offered in this book. The nature of water is included in what it is to be God, on my view. But Leftow has a deep intuition that there is something wrong with finding secular truths encoded in what it is to be God. The truth that water is $H_2O$ is usually taken to be a necessary truth. Whatever else it means to be a necessary truth, it means that not even God could make it false or untrue that water is $H_2O$. This bothers Leftow. Consider that the view I endorse entails that *if* God exists, *then* water is $H_2O$. But by the logical inference rule called '*modus tollens*', it follows that *if* it is not the case that water is $H_2O$, *then* God does not exist.[116]

Now Leftow thinks that it is necessary that water is $H_2O$, so his concern is not that chemists might discover they were wrong about the chemical composition of water and thereby zap God out of existence. Instead, the concern is that God's existence should not depend in any way on secular things. But the conditional that *if* it is not the case that water is $H_2O$, *then* God does not exist sure looks like God's existence depends on the nature of water. But since the chemical composition of water is a purely secular fact, it should be irrelevant to God being what God is. By making the nature of water in some important sense up to God, a product of God's creative thinking not entailed by his thinking about his own nature, Leftow manages to divorce God's nature from the creaturely realm and preserve God's ultimacy.

While I share Leftow's motivation for divine ultimacy, I do not share his intuition that secular truths, even necessary secular truths, threaten divine ultimacy. A better way to put this is that I deny that there are secular truths.

---

[115] Leftow, *God and Necessity*, p. 27.    [116] Leftow, *God and Necessity*, pp. 209–214.

Water is pretty important in Christian theology. Baptism requires water. Water flowed with blood from the side of the crucified Christ. And "there is a river whose streams make glad the city of God, the holy habitation of the Most High (Ps. 46:4)." On my view, water is expressive of what God is. Everything is expressive of what God is. We grasp very little of all this, and we grasp less through discursive methods than through poetic and contemplative methods. But our poor ability to access the distinctive divine expression of each creature is no knock against the God who is the origin of each creature. Creaturely water is a creature, imaging divine water. If God is to each creature as exemplar to image, then Leftow's concern about water just dries up. All the dappled things God fathers forth whose beauty is past change: Praise him.[117]

## 8.5 Representational Artwork

That there are no secular truths should matter a great deal to us. We inhabit a world inescapably divine. Of course, this does not mean that the world is God, or God's body. It means merely that everything in the world resembles its divine archetype. The world is God's artwork and it is inescapably representational artwork.

The problem with representational artworks – I mean those artworks made by humans – is that they tempt us to think that they represent the world as it is, when of course they can only represent the world as it is to us. Things must always mean more than they seem, for things, insofar as they manifest God's own thoughts and God's own nature, have, in MacDonald's words, "layer upon layer of ascending significance."[118] It is no skepticism to admit our limitations. We only see from one perspective at a time. We cannot really even so much as picture to ourselves seeing from all perspectives at once, a single object seen simultaneously from 360 degrees. Braque and Picasso in their Cubist phases tried, but they could not succeed. This is why Cubist paintings look so weird and ugly. I doubt God finds things so weird and ugly when he sees them as the Cubists tried to see them. The attempt to gain a God's eye view severs us from the only means we have to make sense of the world – however little sense that might be.

The human attempt to see the world with nonhuman eyes has produced some monstrosities, some curiosities, even some beauties, but it is no secret to say that art in the twentieth century was driven more than anything else by the pursuit of oddness and novelty. But the containment exemplarist theory of divine ideas helps us see that there really is nothing new under the sun, not because the sun has been around so long but because everything under the sun represents the

---

[117] Hopkins, "Pied Beauty," p. 74.     [118] MacDonald, "The Fantastic Imagination," p. 320.

eternal God who is beyond the stars. Small and happy people like me can enjoy art which is obvious because we know our place in the cosmos: one line of sight at a time, and what a sight to see!

But art which is not at all obvious to me is obvious to God, and this is a problem for ambitious artists. We cannot really move beyond representation in art, though many have tried. Here, just some splatters; there, just some fields of color. But God has beat you to it, Jackson Pollock and Mark Rothko. The exemplar of all color and all geometry, he beholds in himself every conceivable configuration.[119] Perhaps the problem is not representation but art itself. Perhaps we can do art new if we redefine what it means for an artwork to belong to an artist. See this urinal? It is not a urinal. It is a fountain and it is art. You are getting on to something, Marcel Duchamp: everything is art, but however famous you became, it was never really your artwork. Nothing real is truly ours. Then why not take the bold move to make art of that which is not? You may try to crowd out God for four minutes and thirty-three seconds, but it will be only a hole in the fabric of his sound. You may try to pass off a framed piece of blank paper as a drawing, but this will only highlight the hard reality which is paper. John Cage and Gianni Motti, consider the Psalmist: "Whither shall I go from thy Spirit? Or whither shall I flee from thy presence (Ps. 139:7)?" It turns out that if the business of art is novelty then art must turn against God himself, for God keeps art not only intelligible, but old-fashioned. Piss Christ, then, retorts Andres Serrano. But, young man, "Are you able to drink the cup that I drink, or to be baptized with the baptism with which I am baptized (Mk. 10:38)?" God is there even down to the yellow dregs of our rebellion.

## 8.6 Theophany

Recognizing the divine artistry behind all things helps make some sense out of a common human experience: a sense of seeing things as signs, as pointing beyond themselves to some other, less accessible reality. Because we can never know everything God meant in creation, we ought to be open to the discovery, or revelation, of "layer upon layer of ascending significance" in every creature, an openness on display when Joanna Newsom sings, "There are some mornings when the sky feels like a road,"[120] or when Brandi Carlile sings of the time when "the midnight moon shines so bright/Nearly pulled us up to Heaven/By the strings of our heart."[121] What we love when we love a thing which is not God is

---

[119] Coyle, "Creation Anticipated," p. 295.
[120] Joanna Newsom, "Clam, Crab, Cockle, Cowerie," *The Milk-Eyed Mender.*
[121] Brandi Carlile, "Josephine," *The Story.*

both that thing and God, or that part of God which that creature specially resembles. A bush really is a bush, but it is a burning bush.

Samuel Taylor Coleridge eventually came to see that he was wrong when he wrote that "we receive but what we give, / And in our life alone does Nature live."[122] He was wrong because we receive only what God gives, and so by means of Nature we get a glimpse of God. But Coleridge was right to recognize that the world is, after all, essentially implicated in what it is to be personal. For what it does to us, or at least to so many of us, is to make us think that it is whispering secret things about itself and about something beyond itself. If you become convinced it is not disclosing divine things then you must explain away the whispers. Coleridge's response was to conclude, for a time anyway, that he himself was the only mind which spoke through Nature, and, well, this dejected him. Eventually he would find peace by embracing Christianity, which taught him to see our own representations of the natural world as "a repetition in the finite mind of the eternal act of creation in the infinite I AM."[123]

Ultimately, the whispers of roses and yew trees and waterfalls are not enough, because these things are not articulate enough about divine things to be our savior. Or perhaps they just cannot say enough about divine things in a language we can understand. The Incarnation of the Logos might be understood, then, as the act which translates their meaning,[124] a translation performed by the author himself, ensuring the significance of creatures – that is, their ability *to signify.*

This religious significance of all creatures is neatly correlated with the monotheistic impulse against idols. It would be a mean thing for God to demand all our love in a way that required total indifference to or rejection of our creaturely attachments. We were not made to bear that sort of spiritual burden. But if every creature is a little theophany, then the religious life is not a matter of transferring our love from creatures to God, but ordering our love of creatures toward our love for God. And this matters not only for ethics but also for eschatology: an ever-deepening revelation of God in created things asymptotically approaches vision of the divine essence itself, keeping continuity, always, between the loves we never truly leave behind and the Love which is our final end. After Narnia, New Narnia, and therefore closer to the Lion.[125] A religious monotheist should therefore welcome a theory which, if true, made good sense out of the religious sensibilities that God is to be loved above all, but that all things may also be loved, because they may be found in God.

---

[122] Coleridge, "Dejection: An Ode," ll. 47–48.

[123] Coleridge, *Biographia Literaria*, vol. I, pp. 304–305. Guite, *Mariner*, pp. 399–404.

[124] McIntosh, "The Maker's Meaning."     [125] Lewis, *The Last Battle*, pp. 206–211.

# Appendix

Decision Tree for Some Varieties of Abstractionism and Theories of Divine Ideas:

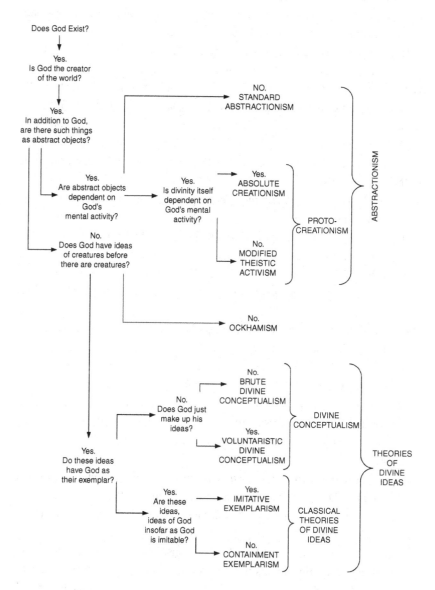

# References

Aertsen, Jan A. *Medieval Philosophy as Transcendental Thought: From Philip the Chancellor (ca. 1225) to Francisco Suárez*. Leiden: Brill, 2012.

Al-Ghazali, *Incoherence of the Philosophers*, trans. Sabih Ahmad Kamali. Lahore: Pakistan Philosophical Congress, 1963.

Allen, James P. *Genesis in Egypt: the Philosophy of Egyptian Creation Accounts*. New Haven, CT: Yale Egyptological Studies 2, 1988.

Anderson, James A. and Welty, Greg. "The Lord of Non-Contradiction: An Argument for God from Logic," *Philosophia Christi* 13:2 (2011), pp. 321–339.

Anselm. *Basic Writings*, ed. and trans. Thomas Williams. Indianapolis, IN: Hackett, 2007.

Aquinas, Thomas. *Basic Works*, ed. Jeffrey Hause and Robert Pasnau. Indianapolis, IN: Hackett, 2014.

Aquinas, Thomas. *Scriptum super Sententiis*. Textum Parmae, 1856. www .corpusthomisticum.org.

Aquinas, Thomas. *Summa theologiae*, 3 vols., trans. The Fathers of the English Dominican Province. New York: Benziger Brothers, 1947.

Arnold, Bill T. and Beyer, Bryan E. *Readings from the Ancient Near East: Primary Sources for Old Testament Study*. Grand Rapids, MI: Baker, 2002.

Assmann, Jan. *Of God and Gods: Egypt, Israel, and the Rise of Monotheism*. Madison, WI: University of Wisconsin Press, 2008.

Assmann, Jan. *The Search for God in Ancient Egypt*, trans. David Lorton. Ithaca, NY: Cornell University Press, 1984.

Augustine. *The City of God Against the Pagans*, trans. R. W. Dyson. Cambridge: Cambridge University Press, 1998.

Augustine. *Confessions*, trans. Henry Chadwick. Oxford: Oxford University Press, 1991.

Augustine. *Eighty-Three Different Questions*, trans. David L. Mosher. Washington, DC: The Catholic University of America Press, 1977.

Augustine. *On Free Choice of the Will*, trans. Thomas Williams. Indianapolis, IN: Hackett, 1993.

Avicenna. *The Metaphysics of The Healing*, trans. Michael E. Marmura. Provo, UT: Brigham Young University Press, 2005.

Bergmann, Michael and Brower, Jeffrey E. "A Theistic Argument Against Platonism (and in Support of Truthmakers and Divine Simplicity)," *Oxford Studies in Metaphysics* 2 (2006), pp. 357–386.

Blander, Josh. "Same as it never was: John Duns Scotus' Paris Reportatio account of identity and distinction," British Journal of the History of Philosophy (2019), pp. 1–20. doi:10.1080/09608788.2019.1624946.

Bonaventure. *Commentary on the Sentences: Philosophy of God*, trans. R. E. Houser and Timothy B. Noone. St. Bonaventure, NY: Franciscan Institute Publications, 2013.

Bonaventure. *Disputed Questions on the Knowledge of Christ*, trans. Zachary Hayes, OFM. St. Bonaventure, NY: Franciscan Institute Publications, 2005.

Burkert, Walter. *Babylon, Memphis, Persepolis: Eastern Contexts of Greek Culture*. Cambridge, MA: Harvard University Press, 2004.

Carlile, Brandi. *The Story*. Columbia Records, 2007.

Carson, D. A. *The Gospel According to John*. Grand Rapids: Eerdmans, 1991.

Clouser, Roy A. *The Myth of Religious Neutrality: An Essay on the Hidden Role of Religious Belief in Theories*. Notre Dame, IN: University of Notre Dame Press, 2005.

Coleridge, Samuel Taylor. *Biographia Literaria*, ed. James Engell and W. Jackson Bate. Princeton: Princeton University Press, 1983.

Coleridge, Samuel Taylor. *The Complete Poems*, ed. William Keach. London: Penguin, 1997.

Copenhaver, Brian P. *Hermetica: The Greek Corpus Hermeticum and the Latin Asclepius in a new English translation, with Notes and Introduction*. Cambridge: Cambridge University Press, 1992.

Coyle, Justin Shaun, "Creation Anticipated: Maximian Reverberations in Bonaventure's Exemplarism," in *Maximus the Confessor as a European Philosopher*, ed. Sotiris Mitralexis, Georgios Steiris, Marcin Podbielski, and Sebastian Lalla. Eugene, OR: Cascade Books, 2017, pp. 284–303.

Craig, William Lane. *God Over All: Divine Aseity and the Challenge of Platonism*. Oxford: Oxford University Press, 2016.

Cross, Richard. *Duns Scotus on God*. London: Routledge, 2005.

Cross, Richard. "Gregory of Nyssa on Universals," *Vigiliae Christianiae* 56:4 (2002), pp. 372–410.

Descartes. *Meditations, Objections, and Replies*, ed. and trans. Roger Ariew and Donald Cress. Indianapolis, IN: Hackett, 2006.

Dillon, John. *The Middle Platonists: 80 B.C. To A.D. 220*, rev. ed. Ithaca, NY: Cornell University Press, 1996.

Dillon, John. *The Roots of Platonism: The Origins and Chief Features of a Philosophical Tradition*. Cambridge: Cambridge University Press, 2019.

Dionysius [Pseudo.]. *The Divine Names and The Mystical Theology*, trans. John D. Jones. Milwaukee, WI: Marquette University Press, 2011.

Duns Scotus, John. *The Examined Report of the Paris Lecture: Reportatio I-A*, 2 vols., ed. and trans. Allan B. Wolter and Oleg V. Bychkov. St. Bonaventure, NY: St. Bonaventure University Press, 2008.

Duns Scotus, John. *Ordinatio, in Opera Omnia*, vols.I–XIV, ed. The Scotistic Commission. Vatican City: Typis Vaticanis, 1950–2013.

Duns Scotus, John. *Philosophical Writings*, trans. Allan Wolter. Indianapolis, IN: Hackett, 1987.

Duns Scotus, John. *A Treatise on God as First Principle*, trans. and ed. Allan B. Wolter. Chicago: Franciscan Herald Press, 1966.

Farrer, Austin. *Faith and Speculation: An Essay in Philosophical Theology*. London: Adam and Charles Black, 1967.

Faulkner, R. O. *The Ancient Egyptian Pyramid Texts*. Oxford: Oxford University Press, 1969.

Foster, John L. *Hymns, Prayers, and Songs: An Anthology of Ancient Egyptian Lyric Poetry*, ed. Susan Tower Hollis. SBL Writings from the Ancient World 8. Atlanta: Scholars Press, 1995.

Frost, Gloria. "Thomas Aquinas on the Perpetual Truth of Essential Propositions," *History of Philosophy Quarterly* 27:3 (2010), pp. 197–213.

Gersh, Stephen. *From Iamblichus to Eriugena: An Investigation of the Prehistory and Evolution of the Pseudo-Dionysian Tradition*. Leiden: Brill, 1978.

Gould, Paul. *Beyond the Control of God? Six Views on the Problem of God and Abstract Objects*. New York: Bloomsbury, 2014.

Guite, Malcom. *Mariner: A Voyage with Samuel Taylor Coleridge*. London: Hodder & Stoughton, 2017.

Heidel, Alexander. *The Babylonian Genesis: the Story of Creation*, 2nd ed. Chicago: University of Chicago Press, 1951.

Henry of Ghent. *Summae Quaestionum Ordinariarum*, 2 vols. Paris, 1520. Rpt. St. Bonaventure, NY: The Franciscan Institute, 1953.

Hoffmeier, James K. *Akhenaten and the Origins of Monotheism*. Oxford: Oxford University Press, 2017.

Hopkins, Gerard Manley. *Poems*, 3rd ed., ed. W. H. Gardner. London: Oxford University Press, 1948.

Hornung, Erik. *Conceptions of God in Ancient Egypt: The One and the Many*, trans. John Baines. Ithaca, NY: Cornell University Press, 1982.

Klima, Gyula. "The Medieval Problem of Universals", The Stanford Encyclopedia of Philosophy (Winter 2017), ed. Edward N. Zalta. https://plato .stanford.edu/archives/win2017/entries/universals-medieval/.

Klocker, Harry R. "Ockham and the Divine Ideas," *The Modern Schoolman* 57:4 (1980), pp. 348–360.

Kretzmann, Norman. *The Metaphysics of Creation: Aquinas's Natural Theology in* Summa Contra Gentiles II. Oxford: Clarendon Press, 1998.

Kripke, Saul. "A Completeness Theorem in Modal Logic," *The Journal of Symbolic Logic* 24:1 (1959), pp. 1–14.

Kripke, Saul. *Naming and Necessity*. Oxford. Basil Blackwell, 1980.

Lambert, W. G. *Babylonian Creation Myths*. Winona Lake, IN: Eisenbraums, 2013.

LaZella, Andrew. *The Singular Voice of Being: John Duns Scotus and Ultimate Difference*. New York: Fordham University Press, 2019.

Leftow, Brian. *God and Necessity*. Oxford: Oxford University Press, 2012.

Leibniz, Gottfried Wilhelm. *Discourse on Metaphysics*, trans. Roger Ariew and Daniel Garber, in Leibniz, Philosophical Essays. Indianapolis, IN: Hackett, 1989, pp. 35–68.

Lewis, C. S. *The Last Battle*. New York: HarperTrophy, 1994.

Lewis, C. S. *The Voyage of the Dawn Treader, in The Chronicles of Narnia*. New York: Harper Collins, 2004, pp. 419–542.

Lewis, David. *On the Plurality of Worlds*. Oxford: Blackwell Publishing, 1986.

Lichtheim, Miriam. *Ancient Egyptian Literature Volume I: The Old and Middle Kingdoms*. Berkeley: University of California Press, 1973.

Lovejoy, A. O. *The Great Chain of Being: A Study of the History of an Idea*. New York: Harper & Brothers, 1960.

MacDonald, George. "The Fantastic Imagination," in *A Dish of Orts: Chiefly Papers on the Imagination, and on Shakespere [sic]*, enlarged ed. London: Sampson Low Marston & Company, 1895, pp. 313–322.

Majercik, Ruth. *The Chaldean Oracles*, 2nd ed. Bream, England: The Prometheus Trust, 2013.

Marrone, Steven P. "Revisiting Duns Scotus and Henry of Ghent on Modality," in *John Duns Scotus: Metaphysics and Ethics*, ed. Ludger Honnefelder, Rega Wood, and Mechthild Dreyer. Leiden: Brill, 1996, pp. 175–189.

Marrone, Steven P. *Truth and Scientific Knowledge in the Thought of Henry of Ghent*. Cambridge, MA: Medieval Academy of America, 1985.

Maximus the Confessor. *On Difficulties in the Church Fathers: The Ambigua*, 2 vols., ed. and trans. Nicholas Constas. Cambridge, MA: Harvard University Press, 2014.

May, Herbert G. and Metzger, Bruce M. *The New Oxford Annotated Bible with the Apocrypha*, expanded edition. Revised Standard Version. New York: Oxford University Press, 1977.

McCann, Hugh J. *Creation and the Sovereignty of God*. Bloomington, IN: Indiana University Press, 2013.

McIntosh, Jonathan. *The Flame Imperishable: Tolkien, St. Thomas, and the Metaphysics of Faërie*. Kettering, OH: Angelico Press, 2017.

McIntosh, Mark, "The Maker's Meaning: Divine Ideas and Salvation," *Modern Theology* 28:3 (2012), pp. 365–384.

McNamara, Martin. *Targum and Testament Revisited: Aramaic Paraphrases of the Hebrew Bible*, 2nd ed. Grand Rapids, MI: Eerdmans, 2010.

Morris, Thomas V. and Menzel, Christopher. "Absolute Creation," *American Philosophical Quarterly* 23:4 (1986), pp. 353–362.

Murphy, Mark C. *God and Moral Law: On the Theistic Explanation of Morality.* Oxford: Oxford University Press, 2011

Murphy, Mark C. *God's Own Ethics: Norms of Divine Agency and the Argument from Evil.* Oxford: Oxford University Press, 2017.

Newson, Joanna. *The Milk-Eyed Mender.* Drag City, 2004.

Ockham, William of. *Scriptum in Librum Primum Sententiarum, Ordinatio: Distinctiones XIX-XLVIII*, ed. Girardus I. Etzkorn and Franciscus E. Kelley. St. Bonaventure, NY: St. Bonaventure University, 2000.

Origen. *On First Principles*, trans. G. W. Butterworth. Notre Dame, IN: Ave Maria Press, 2013

Panchuk, Michelle. "Created and Uncreated Things: A Neo-Augustinian Solution to the Bootstrapping Problem," *International Philosophical Quarterly* 56:1 (2016), pp. 99–112.

Parke-Taylor, G. H. *Yahweh: The Divine Name in the Bible.* Waterloo, Ontario: Wilfrid Laurer University Press, 1975.

Pelletier, Jenny. "William Ockham on Divine Ideas, Universals, and God's Power," in *Universals in the Fourteenth Century*, ed. F. Amerini and L. Cesalli. Pisa: Edizioni della Normale, 2017, pp. 187–224.

Philo of Alexandria, "On the Account of the World's Creation Given by Moses," in Philo, I, trans. F. H. Colson and G. H. Whitaker. *Loeb Classical Library.* Cambridge, MA: Harvard University Press, 1929.

Pickstock, Catherine. "Duns Scotus: His Historical and Contemporary Significance," *Modern Theology* 21:4 (2005), pp. 543–574.

Plantinga, Alvin. "Actualism and Possible Worlds," in Plantinga, *Essays in the Metaphysics of Modality*, ed. Matthew Davidson. Oxford: Oxford University Press, 2003, pp. 103–121.

Plantinga, Alvin. *Does God Have a Nature?* Milwaukee, WI: Marquette University Press, 1980.

Plantinga, Alvin. *God, Freedom, and Evil.* Grand Rapids, MI: Eerdmans, 1974.

Plantinga, Alvin. "How to be an Anti-Realist," *Proceedings and Addresses of the American Philosophical Association* 56:1 (1982), pp. 47–70.

Plantinga, Alvin. *The Nature of Necessity.* Oxford: Clarendon Press, 1974.

Plantinga, Alvin. *Warrant and Proper Function*. Oxford: Oxford University Press, 1993.

Plantinga, Alvin. *Where the Conflict Really Lies: Science, Religion, and Naturalism*. Oxford: Oxford University Press, 2011.

Plato. *Complete Works*, ed. John M. Cooper. Indianapolis, IN: Hackett, 1997.

Plotinus, *The Enneads*, ed. Lloyd P. Gerson, trans. George Boys-Stones, John M. Dillon, Lloyd P. Gerson, R. A. H. King, Andrew Smith, and James Wilberding. Cambridge: Cambridge University Press, 2018.

Proclus, *The Elements of Theology*, 2nd ed. Ed. and trans. E. R. Dodds. Oxford: Clarendon Press, 1962.

Rabinowitz, Jacob. *The Faces of God: Canaanite Mythology as Hebrew Theology*. Woodstock, CT: Spring Publications, 1998.

Reid, Thomas. *Essays on the Active Powers of Man*. Edinburgh: John Bell, 1788.

Ronning, John. *The Jewish Targums and John's Logos Theology*. Peabody, MA: Hendrickson, 2010.

Rosen, Gideon. "Abstract Objects," The Stanford Encyclopedia of Philosophy (Winter 2018), ed. Edward N. Zalta. https://plato.stanford.edu/archives/win2018/entries/abstract-objects/.

Ross, James. "Aquinas's Exemplarism; Aquinas's Voluntarism," *American Catholic Philosophical Quarterly* 64:2 (1990), pp. 171–198.

Seneca. *Ad Lucilium Epistulae Morales*, vol. 1, trans. Richard M. Gummere. London: William Heinemann, 1917.

Smith, Mark. *The Early History of God: Yahweh and the Other Deities in Ancient Israel*, 2nd ed. Grand Rapids, MI: Eerdmans, 2002.

Smith, Mark. *The Origins of Biblical Monotheism: Israel's Polytheistic Background and the Ugaritic Texts*. Oxford: Oxford University Press, 2001.

Spade, Paul Vincent (ed.). *Five Texts on the Mediaeval Problem of Universals: Porphyry, Boethius, Abelard, Duns Scotus, Ockham*, trans. Paul Vincent Space. Indianapolis: Hackett, 1994.

Tolkien, J. R. R. *The Silmarillion*. Boston: Houghton Mifflin, 1977.

van Inwagen, Peter. "God and Other Uncreated Things," in *Metaphysics and the Good: Essays in Honor of Eleonore Stump*, ed. Kevin Timpe. New York: Routledge, 2009, pp. 3–20.

von Balthasar, Hans Urs. *Cosmic Liturgy: The Universe According to Maximus the Confessor*, trans. Brian E. Daly, S.J. San Francisco: Ignatius Press, 2003.

Ward, Thomas M. "Scotism about Possible Natures," *The Philosophical Quarterly* 69:275 (2019), pp. 393–408.

Williams, Thomas and Steele, Jeff. "Complexity without Composition: Duns Scotus on Divine Simplicity," *American Catholic Philosophical Quarterly* 93:4, (2019), pp. 611–631. doi:10.5840/acpq2019920185.

Wippel, John F. "Thomas Aquinas on the Distinction and Derivation of the Many from the One," *Review of Metaphysics* 38:3 (1985), pp. 563–590.

Wittgenstein, Ludwig. *Tractatus Logico-Philosophicus*, trans. C. K. Ogden. London: Kegan Paul, Trench, Trubner & Co., Ltd., 1922.

Wolfson, Harry. *Philo: Foundations of Religious Philosophy in Judaism, Christianity, and Islam*, 2 vols., Cambridge, MA: Harvard University Press, 1962.

Wolter, Allan B. "The Formal Distinction," in Wolter, *The Philosophical Theology of John Duns Scotus*, ed. Marilyn McCord Adams. St. Bonaventure, NY: Franciscan Institute Publications, 2015, pp. 31–48.

# Acknowledgments

This Element is a scratch on the surface of deep things, and I hope to write more in the future which will do a bit more justice to them. I am grateful to Paul Moser and Chad Meister for giving me the opportunity to share my work in this condensed format. I am also grateful to the students in my Spring 2019 seminar on Divine Ideas who helped me think better about this topic; and to my wife, Katie Ward, and two anonymous referees for Cambridge University Press, whose feedback improved the manuscript. I dedicate this Element to John Mark Reynolds, who introduced me to Christian Platonism twenty years ago.

Most of my academic work thus far has been devoted to interpreting philosophical and theological texts written in the Middle Ages, especially those written by John Duns Scotus (d. 1308). This Element features plenty of medieval philosophical theology, and even some Scotus. But this is not an interpretive exercise. I mean it to be a living philosophy, accessible to all philosophically inclined readers, not just academicians. For this reason, I have avoided where possible the jargons of academic philosophy and the academic study of the history of philosophy, and have done my best to explain in plain words all terms which have a jargony whiff. As Charles Williams said somewhere, "Individualiter, essentialiter, categoricorum, differentia substantialis – croak, croak, croak." God forbid.

Cambridge Elements ⁼

# Religion and Monotheism

### Paul K. Moser
*Loyola University Chicago*

**Paul K. Moser** is Professor of Philosophy at Loyola University Chicago. He is the author of *The God Relationship; The Elusive God* (winner of national book award from the Jesuit Honor Society); *The Evidence for God; The Severity of God; Knowledge and Evidence* (all Cambridge University Press); and *Philosophy after Objectivity* (Oxford University Press); co-author of *Theory of Knowledge* (Oxford University Press); editor of *Jesus and Philosophy* (Cambridge University Press) and *The Oxford Handbook of Epistemology* (Oxford University Press); co-editor of *The Wisdom of the Christian Faith* (Cambridge University Press). He is the co-editor with Chad Meister of the book series *Cambridge Studies in Religion, Philosophy, and Society.*

### Chad Meister
*Bethel University*

**Chad Meister** is Professor of Philosophy and Theology and Department Chair at Bethel College. He is the author of *Introducing Philosophy of Religion* (Routledge, 2009), *Christian Thought: A Historical Introduction*, 2nd edition (Routledge, 2017), and *Evil: A Guide for the Perplexed*, 2nd edition (Bloomsbury, 2018). He has edited or co-edited the following: *The Oxford Handbook of Religious Diversity* (Oxford University Press, 2010), *Debating Christian Theism* (Oxford University Press, 2011), with Paul Moser, *The Cambridge Companion to the Problem of Evil* (Cambridge University Press, 2017), and with Charles Taliaferro, *The History of Evil* (Routledge 2018, in six volumes).

### About the Series
This Cambridge Element series publishes original concise volumes on monotheism and its significance. Monotheism has occupied inquirers since the time of the Biblical patriarch, and it continues to attract interdisciplinary academic work today. Engaging, current, and concise, the Elements benefit teachers, researchers, and advanced students in religious studies, Biblical studies, theology, philosophy of religion, and related fields.

Cambridge Elements ☰

# Religion and Monotheism

## Elements in the Series

*Buddhism and Monotheism*
Peter Harvey

*Monotheism and the Meaning of Life*
T. J. Mawson

*Monotheism and Contemporary Atheism*
Michael Ruse

*Monotheism and Hope in God*
William J. Wainwright

*Monotheism and Religious Diversity*
Roger Trigg

*Divine Ideas*
Thomas M. Ward

A full series listing is available at: www.cambridge.org/er&m

Printed in the United States
by Baker & Taylor Publisher Services